Praise for
Building Bridges: Today's Decisions – Gateway to Your Future

"There are many business books, but very few are as practical and provide such a helpful framework for strategic thinking as *Building Bridges*. "

Lauris N. Molbert, Chief Executive Officer
TMI Hospitality

"This book reminds me of *Built to Last* and *Good to Great*, but includes an additional set of ideas. It brings the personal elements – values, ideals, and motivations – to the discussion. *Building Bridges: Today's Decisions – Gateway to Your Future* is a wholly-integrated model that captures the organizational imperatives with the personal imperatives. To achieve long-term success, a leader must incorporate all of these pieces."

D.C. Coston, Ph. D., President
Dickinson State University

"This exceptional book is not only enjoyable, it is immensely valuable. It enabled me to build a bridge to the future and simultaneously a bridge to my heart. I commend it to anyone who seeks a richer life. The bridge metaphor is more than a just a powerful metaphor, it is a parable, in the traditional Biblical sense. I read this book while recuperating in hospital from an unplanned surgery. Very quickly it became a delightful learning experience, with time for me to reflect on my life's journey. Before reading this book I had written in my journal that I wanted to use this surgery as an opportunity to 'start my life anew.' This book was the perfect vehicle for me to reassess my life's direction."

Gerard McMullan, Managing Director
McMullan Peters

"I have known Mel professionally and personally for over a decade and experienced his leadership development work firsthand. His success comes from his ability to model effective leadership. This latest work does a nice job of simplifying critical business concepts with the straightforward, easily understood bridge model."

Eric Michel, P. E., President & CEO
Ulteig Engineers, Inc.

"Over many years I have personally observed Mel Nelson develop the principles for the development of both strategy and leadership. As an executive business leader and a structural engineer, I am impressed with the leadership principles in this book. In *Building Bridges: Today's Decisions – Gateway to Your Future*, Mel has made a direct connection between the structural elements in bridge design and charting a new, exciting vision and strategy for the future."

Brian D. Long, P. E., Executive Vice President
Ulteig Engineers, Inc.

"This book was a blessing for me. I have known Mel for the better part of twenty years and, during that time, I have come to understand his goodness, sincerity and wisdom. This book is a chronicle of a good man's career. Interspersed within its pages are nuggets of knowledge that speak to a career guided by a moral compass. His resolute dedication to his family and purposeful work is an inspiration to those of us who work for more than just a paycheck. Perhaps the most important aspect of the book for me was Mel's admonition that it is impossible to separate personal faith from business; I have struggled with this fact for most of my career. Mel has helped me understand that a truly effective leader embraces the integration of his faith and his role as a leader because his faith is much more than a part of who he is, it is the essence of who he is. The two cannot possibly be separated because, together, they comprise the whole man. Mel, I will be forever grateful."

Vern Dosch, President & Chief Executive Officer
National Information Solutions Cooperative

"Mel Nelson once told me, 'A weak leader deserves the dysfunctional culture he helps to create.' That phrase has challenged me more than once to make difficult yet correct decisions. In *Building Bridges: Today's Decisions – Gateway to Your Future* Mel draws from who he is: engineer, executive, leader, man-of-God. His leadership principles have been an inspiration to me. He defines success as an interdependent synergy of values and choices that find their ultimate expression in organizational health. This book is an actionable blueprint for personal, professional and organizational success. Those building on these foundations will long make journeys of significance."

George Henderson
Executive Director, Top-Quartile Performance Institute

"In a time of trial, Mel's chapter on living life with vision was an inspiration to me. As the company commander of 250 soldiers in Afghanistan, I realized that without the vision to lead myself and my wife first, my company would ultimately suffer without an effective leader. Later, in making the difficult decision to transition out of the military and go back to school to pursue an MBA, I trusted God to guide my path. Building Bridges is an invaluable guide for all stages of life and career."

Mark Herman, Captain, Aviation
4-414th Regiment, USAR

"Mel Nelson, in *Building Bridges: Today's Decisions - Gateway to Your Future*, has created a unique book for individuals and organizations interested in leadership, transition, strategy, branding, ethics, and personal development. He uses the bridge metaphor, along with many different models embedded in the book, to help understand the important dynamics within an organization. His main topics of values, relationships, leadership, and strategy are explained well in the book. The quotes and different sources brought together provide many interesting perspectives and wisdom for anyone interested in building or improving an organization. I highly recommend this professional, well-edited and well-organized book."

James Legler, Ph.D,
Associate Professor of Leadership and Ethics with the Center
for Ethical Leadership, Offutt School of Business
Concordia College

"This is an inspiring and reflective piece for any professional on a journey of reaching higher towards potential actualization. The use of nature and the bridge establishes the concepts shared pictorially in the reader's mind. I agree with Mel's statement that 'Many times efforts to define visionary business strategy fail because the effort is short on commitment of the necessary leadership resources – time, talent, and or energy' and I believe it is also applicable to team formation. The book shows how our personal values influence business model development."

Dr. Lana Adeleye-Olusae
Surefooting

Ron &
KAREN —
GOD BLESS YOU
KEEP
AS YOU
BRIDGES
TO
BUILDING
FROM HERE
ETERNITY!
— MEL & CIA

Building Bridges:

Today's Decisions –
Gateway to Your Future

Melvin D. Nelson

Building Bridges:
Today's Decisions – Gateway to Your Future

Published in the United States of America by
Insight Publishing
Sevierville, Tennessee • www.insightpublishing.com
ISBN 978-1-60013-777-8

Edited by Dave Jameson
Cover Design by Steve Wilson & Jeremy Billups
Interior Format & Design by Dean Lewis
Index by Galen Schroeder

Dedication

This book is dedicated to my wife Cia for the rich memories I have of the last forty-four years ... memories of the numerous bridges to the future we've built together. Many of these bridges we've crossed together ... to what once was the future, but now is the present. Other bridges yet remain ... uncrossed, but still reaching to the future.

Preface

In the summer of 1992, I took my family on an extended motor home trip. Our path stretched from North Dakota, across northern Minnesota, and took us up the North Shore of Lake Superior, with a leg on up into Ontario. With stops at Niagara Falls and other scenic points, our ultimate destination was Washington D.C., where we spent eight days giving our four children a chance to experience our nation's capital firsthand.

Although there were many key points of the trip, one highlight that stands out to this day was our trip across the Mackinac Bridge in Michigan. This is the longest suspension bridge in the western hemisphere and stretches for 26,000 feet – 5.2 miles. Completed over fifty years ago, it has served the state of Michigan well ... and the millions who have crossed the Mackinac Straits on it.

The Mackinac Bridge also has served me well as the metaphor for the work of Executive Management Systems. The model I have developed and used to help my clients to seize opportunities and chart a new path to move their enterprise forward is *"Building Bridges to the Future®."*

Foreword
"For Want of a Bridge ..."

South Sudan is an amazing land stretching across a vast swath of eastern Africa, dotted with tiny villages and beautiful people groups filled with dreams for a dynamic future. Several days' speaking at a simple but strategic pastors' training gathering in the diminutive hamlet called Yabus during the late winter of 2008 more than confirmed these observations for me.

Located just miles from the Ethiopian border and accessible primarily by means of a small plane landing on a rough dirt patch believed to be a runway, Yabus was a living monument to South Sudan's struggle for independence, and a testimony to the suffering and bravery of generations of Sudanese who longed for something greater than jihadist oppression. A casual stroll through the village and the surrounding countryside offered me a glimpse of bullet-ridden buildings, downed Soviet-era helicopters, bomb craters the size of large cars, and scores of spent artillery and bullet casings — silent witnesses to brutality and terror.

The heat was oppressive, even in the dry season of early March. Aside from an occasional gas-powered generator or solar panel, there was no electricity. And there was no running water to be found anywhere, save a fast moving river running through the village called the Yabus River.

On the north side of the river rested the core of the village — dusty streets, a boisterous market area, many mud homes, a simple church, and, of course, a jail. The reality was that the people making up Yabus ranged from eager followers of Jesus to ardent communists to Muslims sympathetic to the government in Khartoum to those who did not care about any of those things but were merely attempting to survive. On the south side of the river was a former military encampment that had originally been a missionary compound resurrected as such once more. It was in this complex of mud huts and concrete buildings that I was sleeping, eating and teaching.

And it was here that a dream was unfolding to build a much needed bridge across the raging Yabus River. It would have to be simple. It would have to be inexpensive. It would have to be put together patiently, over a period of time, particularly considering access to bridge building resources was profoundly limited. But it had to happen. It had to happen so that the people making up the communities on either side of the river could cut down their travel time by hours. It had to happen so that when the rainy season came, those on the south side of the river would no longer be stranded for weeks or months on end because a swollen river would not allow them to take their Toyotas across. It had to happen so that the people of Yabus and the surrounding area could catch a glimpse of the future, where people could be more connected, commerce could develop more forcefully, security could be enhanced, and an appropriate kind of pride could swell the ranks of the local citizenry.

Eli Fader, one of the missionaries serving in Yabus, wrote of the necessity of a bridge joining the two sides of the river. "The name of the bridge is Kubri Waheda or Unity Bridge. It is our desire that this bridge brings peace and unity to the village of Yabus and those in the surrounding area."[1] One important description of the project declared, "Yabus, Sudan and its surrounding area is home to five tribes and 60,000 people. Divided by a river that is impassable for up to six months every year, this bridge will unite the town so that both sides will enjoy access to the clinic, market, and schools all year long."[2] And as a man living even for just a few days among the

---

[1] Eli Fader. "Bridge Celebration." *Unity Bridge.*
<http://yabusbridge.blogspot.com/2009/07/bridge-celebration.html> (30 July 2011).
[2] Ibid.

people of Yabus, I can attest to the necessity of the bridge. At first glance it appears to be a very simple thing — planks and cables stretching across a picturesque stream of water pimpled by large boulders and tiny pools. But what it is in reality is life and dignity and hope. It was a dream unfolding when I was there in 2008. Today Kubri Waheda is a dream that has come true. One cannot overestimate the power of that strategic little bridge spanning a raging chasm in the middle of eastern Africa.

Indeed, one cannot overestimate the power of any bridge.

That is why my friend Mel Nelson's model for effective leadership — Bridges to the Future — is so vital in today's climate. It is a model that invites one to adequately discern the necessity of bridging one side of a chasm to the next. Ours is a world of chasms — cultural, business, religious, educational, and political chasms — that need to be crossed. The moral decline of our societies, the economic realities of today's world, and the geopolitical dynamics of our time are proof enough that chasms beg to be spanned.

Mel's model is one that invites dreams forged on the anvil of understood need. Eli Fader's vision to see a bridge connect the two sides of Yabus began with discernment that it would be exceedingly helpful. He dreamed of what could be accomplished if a bridge replaced isolation and anxiety and fear. He conjured up a vision for what the future could hold for generations that would follow him and his. In a world in which most leaders are reduced to managers who can barely help those they serve survive, we need leaders who dream, who cast vision, who look into the future. Someone has to envision what it would be like to cross the chasms. Mel's book helps the reader deal with that incredible demand.

Mel's model is one that also highlights the character of the bridge builder. Eli Fader and his associates displayed a tremendous measure of patience and fortitude as they sought the construction of the bridge that would span the Yabus River. The ancient statesman Kublai Khan was wise to ask the strategic question of any bridge, "Which is the stone that supports the bridge?"[3] No doubt he was thinking of the physical structure itself, that one keystone that provided the structural integrity of the whole. But every bridge requires that figurative stone whose force of character makes the building of it happen — the dreamer, the designer, the individual determined to see it built. Leaders need to be that "stone that supports the bridge," the men and women who make dreams reality, who direct people toward a preferred future, who call us to span the chasms. Mel is one of those leaders, and his work helps us to join his ranks.

Read carefully. Be inspired. Take hold of the call which is exceptional leadership for a chasm-ridden era. As you do you too will become part of that group of leaders building bridges to a future greater than the past while compelling those who follow to look forward with confidence.

Dr. Matthew R. St. John
Teaching Pastor, Bethel Church
Fargo, N.D.

---

[3] "Kublai Khan." BrainyQuote.com.
<http://www.brainyquote.com/quotes/quotes/k/kublaikhan262411.html> (30 July 2011).

Introduction

Building a bridge to the future starts with personal leadership – personal leadership that is anchored in strong values, personal leadership that is supported by strong interpersonal relationships. These personal relationships are based on the bedrock principles of integrity, honesty, and trustworthiness, coupled with a healthy dose of self-awareness and other-awareness – solid emotional intelligence.

This book is about the Building Bridges to the Future® model I've developed over a career focused on defining strategy for teams and corporations. This is a book about process. It focuses on the process of developing business strategy. It also highlights the personal process of developing life strategies ... all in the context of *Building Bridges to the Future®*.

This book is not only about business strategy. It is also about the personal path I've traveled in my life and career as I have developed valuable insight and breakthrough perspective while spending nearly three decades in the energy and telecommunications businesses. Building Bridges to the Future® is not only a business model, it is a life model. It is the product of all my experiences, both in life and business.

At the 2010 Leadership Summit, hosted by the Willow Creek Association, Founder Bill Hybels, in his keynote address spoke of his new book *The Power of a Whisper*. It offers a useful challenge. When we hear God whisper – through his word, circumstances, an idea, our thoughts, other people – what do we do with it? Do we listen to those whispers, reflect, and act? Or do we brush them off as merely a gentle breeze and do nothing? This book, the career opportunities I've had and the life I've lived are the outcome of the many whispers I've heard over the years.

Table of Contents

Chapter One

Seizing Opportunities

Carpe Diem. Seize the day.

"Whatever your hand finds to do, do it with all your might. ..."
– Solomon

This book is a direct outcome of that action strategy – "Seize the day!" By stitching together the opportunities we seize each day, we weave the fabric of our life.

As a young child, I learned from my mother and father to seize opportunities – not passively, but aggressively. My father was a laid-back, take-charge guy (Isn't that contrast in a person a wonderful quality?) who loved people. Throughout his long life, he had a track record of seizing opportunities. My mother was a very intelligent woman who had great language skills and had a lot of knowledge about many things ... and a competitive edge. Both of my parents contributed to my drive to seize opportunities, and this became a key part of my character as a young boy.

In life, we can seize opportunities to develop our personal talent ... or let them pass. In business, we stitch a corporate fabric with the opportunities we seize ... or miss.

Opportunities Seized

When I was ten, we emigrated from Canada to the U.S., halfway through my fifth-grade year. I was thrust into a totally new education curriculum in January, including a U.S. history course.

The Daughters of the American Revolution organization (the D.A.R.) gave awards to fifth-grade students who showed an "outstanding knowledge of U.S. history". It was my mother who encouraged me to use my God-given talents as a student to seize this as an opportunity to excel by mastering the content and memorizing the facts. That spring, three months after crossing the border with my green card, I was one of three students in my school recognized for excellence in knowledge of U.S. history. My mother saw my potential and helped me to draw it out by encouraging me to intensively study the U.S. history material for the test.

With my abilities and interest in math and science, I determined by the ninth grade that I would be an electrical engineer. Throughout my high school years, I continued to seize opportunities for personal growth, continuing to pursue and develop a broad interest in math, science, history, English, speech, psychology, literature, while being on the varsity swimming team. I pursued the same breadth in my education while in engineering. One of my remarkable life experiences – though consistent with my earlier pursuit of a broad education – began in the spring of my sophomore year when I approached the dean of electrical engineering at the University. "Ed, I think too many engineers do not get a broad education," I told him. "I'm looking at all those technical electives we're supposed to take. I'd rather take history, English, business law, psychology, literature, and speech. What do you think?"

He responded by crafting an opportunity that I seized: "The accreditation committee will probably give me a bad time, but I'll tell them you were a good student and I thought it would be good for your education. You can take anything you want from the curriculum." The value of my university education was compounded by his action. Ed had been a captain in the Army Air Corps in WWII and knew that the difference between a medal and a court martial was a very fine line. As dean, he was fully willing to use his position to create the climate and opportunities to allow self-motivated students to excel.

During my senior year at the University, I had numerous employment opportunities throughout the U.S. I chose to remain in the Midwest to seize a young coed's hand in marriage and begin my career while she finished her education. I went to work for Northwestern Bell Telephone. After a year and a half with NWB, I took a year to readjust my course and went to seminary in Deerfield, Illinois as a special student – which allowed me to choose any courses I wished from the curriculum. After two quarters in that rich learning environment, I launched a career in the energy industry which spanned twenty-nine years.

Personal Vision

After fifteen years in that career, I had a vision to start a management consulting business. One of the early steps I took to start the business was to register the trade name Executive Management Systems with the Secretary of State's office in 1986. I chose the name Executive Management Systems because it nailed my business focus:

1. I wanted to focus on the development of leadership strategies at the top; and
2. I wanted to have a bench of models, applications, resources, or "systems" which could be applied to the specific needs of clients.

This choice of focus was a foundational business strategy based on bedrock and proven principles.

In this timeframe (1986-1987), I read Charles Swindoll's book *Living Above the Level of Mediocrity*. The basic point of this book is that we were not created to grovel in mediocrity, but to soar ... live life with vision ... see what most people miss ... let that vision guide our choices and actions.

The French author Victor Hugo spoke to the power of leveraging vision: *"Greater than a mighty army is an idea whose time has come ..."* But the time was not yet ripe for me to launch the business I envisioned. I had a neat family and was raising neat children – three boys and a girl. I held off pursuing my dream of launching a new business venture. Instead, I chose to continue a full-time career in the energy industry. I had a family to raise with my wife, and I wanted to actively participate. I made the right choice.

My career outlook broadened as I took on more leadership responsibility for marketing and public relations for a progressive regional power supplier. One of the highlights of this time was the opportunity I had to serve on the executive steering committee that created the first national electric energy brand – "Touchstone Energy®" – and then to serve on its first board of directors.

Transition(s)

Transition is a process of travelling a path from "what was" to "what will be." I was working in an industry which focused heavily on tangible assets and not on intangible assets, an industry with a workforce of primarily analytical, logic-driven employees. Throughout the decade of the '90s, marketing and public relations positions in the electric energy industry became a threatened species. The executive position I held was eliminated in 2000.

Professional success can lead to restraint by a set of "golden handcuffs." We can become so comfortable in a career that life on the cutting edge, the exhilaration and excitement of change, escapes us. Our professional lives become a case of "same old / same old." I've heard a rut defined as "a grave with the ends knocked out."

A successful career can become an intellectual prison. Instead of reaching to the horizon with your vision, you look only to the edge of your rut. This type of confining, limiting imprisonment was driven home to me in a humorous way recently when I was listening to a song by Jim Croce – "Stone Walls". It is a song about a man who has been in prison too long and has felt the confinement of the bars and walls. He asks the poignant question, *"Do you feel like there's a shackle around your mind?"*

I was imprisoned in a career that threatened me in a big way. That threat was that I would go to my grave with untapped potential ... personal talent never realized ... dreams never achieved.

Trusting God in Transition

During this time of transition (2000 to 2002), I found that my wife and I went from trusting a corporation for our next paycheck to trusting God for our financial security. It was a time to walk by faith. Every time we took a step, God would provide. The old Irish greeting – *"May the road rise to meet you"* – is a good visual picture of walking by faith, stepping into the unknown before you have solid traction under your feet ... stepping into the abyss of the future, and having a foothold precisely when it is needed to arrest a vertical plunge and to support forward progress.

During this transition, I had twenty-one months of contract work with a start-up telecom. Following that, I searched for other executive opportunities and I held one other executive position.

In December 2002 I incorporated Executive Management Systems and launched the business with a passion. This passion had been building over a career which spanned more than thirty years.

As I seized this opportunity to launch the business, I had to build a business strategy and brand identity around the personal talent which I had developed and fine-tuned over this business career.

Building a Business

After three decades of immersion in progressive learning about leadership and strategy development in business, I now had the opportunity for a big stakes application – How would I develop an executive consulting practice?

The business name – Executive Management Systems – focuses on my target market. With the years of executive suite and boardroom exposure I'd had throughout my career, a fundamental strategy for my business was to start at the top. Another fundamental strategy – this business would be built on a foundation of relationships – strong ties on a personal, ethical and relational level. A given for those at the top is the loneliness of high command. Often, one of my key roles in consulting is to take up a position as the CEO's wingman and fly formation as we develop strategy together.

The executive consulting business I envisioned would offer a broad range of services which would be tailored to meet the specific client needs. The solid relationships and breadth of solutions would encourage in-depth, long-term relationships with clients to develop long-term solutions to their pressing problems.

To ensure the depth of bench and variety of solutions, I would develop a network of national and international contacts. This would ensure the necessary on-going talent development for me personally. The major strategic investments I knew I would make would not be in tangible assets – they would be in the intangible assets of professional knowledge, and developing a stimulating network of professional colleagues was absolutely essential to my success.

I deliberately chose to develop professional credentials to allow me to compete on a national level, but deliberately chose to focus on developing a strong regional presence. In my view, travel time is not productive time. My target market is within four hours' travel of my office.

Another fundamental choice I made was to operate without debt – to build the business on the principle of financial freedom. I also chose to develop a substantial financial operating reserve. These fundamental choices have served me very well.

When it comes to business planning for Executive Management Systems, I firmly believe the principle of "Go as far as you can see ... and when you get there, you can see further." This, too, is another fundamental choice that has served me well. It frees me up from having to have everything figured out before I pull the trigger on decisions. Another key planning principle which has worked well is a three-year planning cycle. A three-year planning horizon is close enough that we can begin to see it. We have to take action today to accomplish significant results in three years. A three-year timeframe creates an opportunity to launch major business development strategy a step at a time, with distinct benchmarks to be set and achieved along the way. I've surprised myself in the way that stretch goals set three years out have been achieved. Executive Management Systems is now in its tenth year of operation since incorporation. I've had three full three-year cycles of planning, and I will move the cheese again in January of 2012.

Developing a Brand Identity

As I mentioned earlier, I had to build a business strategy and brand identity around the talent I had developed and fine-tuned over my professional business career. The brand definition, brand values and brand equity of a sole consultancy are inextricably entwined with the personal style, talents and skills of the principal. This ensuing discussion is not about building ego. It is about developing insight into the brand promise of Executive Management Systems, Inc.

As individual human beings, we are often unaware of some of our greatest strengths. The reason for this is that we are blinded by our ego-centric point of view. We do not recognize our talent as unique and distinctive ... because we think everyone is just like us ... and we think that they have the same talents we do. We need others to help us bust this enslaving paradigm to bring an accurate awareness of our talent and skills into focus – that uniqueness which ultimately drives our competitive advantage as business leaders.

This is not unlike the "blinding" of a celestial observatory by the light pollution in the night sky when telescopes are located too close to metropolitan areas. Astronomers know they must choose a remote, darker locale to clearly see the light from distant stars. By the same token, we personally need to step back from the ego-centric glare we all suffer from and let others' perceptions of our unique strengths guide our thinking and personal professional development.

Stephen Covey cautions us about paying too much attention to the "social mirror" which he describes as "the opinions, perceptions, and paradigms of the people around us."[4] But it has been my

---

[4] Stephen R. Covey, *The 7 Habits of Highly Effective People* (New York: Simon & Schuster, 1989), p. 67.

experience that the social mirror has been a very valuable and priceless source of insight for me as I have developed my personal abilities and refined my talent to deliver business solutions.

It is my firm conviction that: Consulting talent is identified, developed and finely honed by being especially sensitive to others.

On the other hand, there is an important caveat I should mention: "Pay attention to your critics ... but don't let them steer your ship." I've always reserved the right to employ a "Take it or leave it" approach to feedback. This is because of the truth of what a wizened sergeant from the Korean War once told me: "Mel, my boy, there's a fine line between constructive criticism and cheap harassment."

Cheap harassment – internalized – leads to self-doubt. Constructive criticism – dealt with directly and creatively – leads to confidence in building a better future.

To more sharply define my personal brand identity, I reflected on my career of three decades. In 2001, I asked a half dozen professional business associates who knew me well over the long haul – three decades – to answer two questions:

Key question – "If you were to brand Mel Nelson as a product, what qualities would you promote?" To say it another way – "What are the attributes in Mel Nelson as a professional which bring high value to the organization?"

From this exercise came a list of nine talents / personal qualities that they used to define me:
- Communication
- Decision-maker
- Experienced, knowledgeable & well-read
- Innovation

- Integrity
- Leadership
- Relationships
- Strategic thinking
- Teamwork

While I was receiving this feedback, there were some real growth moments for me. One occurred when I was told that I was totally honest. I was a bit taken aback. Why was that a defining quality? Isn't everyone honest? What's so unusual about that? This was the first of many experiences that showed me how blind we are to our unique strengths because we think everyone is just like us. I thought about that feedback on honesty for three days before the reality set in: It's rare to experience total honesty.

These discussions were very useful to me when I incorporated Executive Management Systems, Inc. in 2002, and began to define the "brand promise". How well would I execute? How well would I stand and deliver? This wasn't an idle thought, nor was it a passing concern. Ninety percent of start-up consulting firms fail within the first two years.

One fact which gave me great confidence in launching this business was my three decades of professional business and leadership experience. I knew that, "Experience is a better education than a college degree ... but the tuition is higher." The life and business acumen I had acquired the hard way gave me the perspective and confidence to be successful in executive consulting. This confidence was reinforced by a Tom Clancy book I was reading at the time. Clancy's first non-fiction work, an "account of transformations," it documented the leadership challenges of Operation Desert Storm, as seen through the eyes of General Fred Franks, commander of the VII Corps armor and infantry. "Normally it takes from twenty-eight to thirty years of experience, personal study, demonstrated competence, education, and training to develop a corps commander. A division commander normally has twenty-two to twenty-five years. Brigade commanders from twenty to twenty-two years."[5] No question about it. I had the experience to do what I intended to do. And that built my confidence. My experience molded and shaped my brand identity.

"Work Your Magic"

The brand promise of Executive Management Systems, the unique value proposition, has been continually and gradually refined in contact with clients as I have learned of the value I bring to the table. The following story illustrates this point.

One of the clients I'd worked with on several occasions was a telecommunications company. One of the board members described my assignment, "Mel, we want you to come and work your magic." Over the years, I've come to develop a deep appreciation for what he meant when he said that. It means creating an atmosphere where people can speak up. It means a focus on present moment awareness, not jumping ahead to what comes next ... patiently letting the plot or theme develop. It means affirming individuals and valuing their every contribution to the discussion. It means withholding premature judgment on ideas. It means drawing out those who often say little because they're overrun by those who are impatient, loud, boisterous, pushy. It means valuing people for their uniqueness. It means high-energy listening. It means paying attention to the language ... their language. It means combining all of their ideas and synthesizing them into a natural hierarchy of thought. It means crafting strategy from their words. It means alignment, clarity, and engagement. It results in action.

---

[5] Tom Clancy, with General Fred Franks, Jr. (Ret.), *Into the Storm: A Study in Command* (New York: G.P. Putnam's Sons, 1997) p. 165.

Three stories further illustrate this "magic." I was engaged with one client in a day-long strategy session with a board. One of the board members was a university president who thanked me at the end of the day for my work and commented, "You're so affirming. People can say anything they want and it's OK with you." I took it as a compliment and thanked her. But over the weekend, I thought about this comment and asked myself, "So what? What's the implication of that?" So I called her the next week out of curiosity, to gain further understanding. She reflected thoughtfully for a moment and then said, "Your affirmation of others generates instant respect. And respect builds trust. And trust is huge." Another executive underscored that thought when he said, "100% trust was achieved between board and management" through in-depth discussion of their issues.

In another setting, I was engaged to do a session on project management in a leadership development curriculum with two dozen participants. Immediately after the session, the client told me, "Mel, I was amazed at how quickly you engaged the entire group. You called them each by name, related to them individually. You used a variety of ways to acknowledge the wisdom in the group: 'That's a perfect fit with what we're talking about.' You affirmed their knowledge and encouraged their participation. It's a wonderful skill – to take the words of the audience, to make them fit together in a remarkable way. You're skilled enough to see it and take it to the next step."

Another CEO put it this way, "Stepping in to guide conversation, stepping back to let the board take the initiative, bringing the board to a synopsis of their thinking. Most facilitators cannot do that. It's a real talent. This has really accelerated our strategic thinking. We're six months ahead of where I thought we'd be."

A board member from another business said, "You drew out the board's thinking in a couple of board sessions and put structure to a thought process we had been tap-dancing around for a year."

One of the stories I like to tell which further underscores what I do is about the ski trips we used to take with our kids and friends. One of my buddies, who particularly liked to ski is a dentist. The most important moving parts of a dentist are thumb and forefingers – to grip appliances, tools, patients, whatever – in the practice of dentistry. The most frequent injury of skiers is a dislocated thumb, caused by falling with the ski poles.

It seemed that on every ski trip, my buddy would come back with hand, thumb, or finger injuries. On one trip, after a run through the trees, he came out the other side with the index finger of his left hand at a ninety degree angle the wrong way. In the emergency room, he had three or four ER attendants holding his hand and arm and pulling on his finger to try to get the finger back into its normal position. They were making no progress and indicated that the next option was surgery. My pal insisted they consult with an orthopedic surgeon. He came and with gentle manipulation of the ligaments and joint of that finger, was able to pop it back into its proper position.

I use that illustration in describing my work to develop business strategy in a team setting: Many times, all of the essentials are there. We merely have to gently massage the concepts until the proper strategy "pops" ... and it comes clearly into focus.

Creating a Brand

In addition to developing a brand promise, an important part of creating a brand identity is to have a sharp business-to-business presence that is created and enabled by first-class graphics – a logo that cuts through the clutter. Although a brand is much more than a logo, a solid brand is well-served by an effective logo.

Three years before I incorporated Executive Management Systems, I worked through several concepts with a talented graphic artist to develop a strong graphic element to project a strong business-to-business image. Having already worked through the key elements of a business focus, this was a relatively easy exercise.

The logo developed is distinctive, memorable, and effective. It's a strong business-to-business communications strategy. Because it has served me well, it has been trademarked:

In September of 2004, I attended a conference in Las Vegas sponsored by one of my consulting networks. One of the first individuals I met was a colleague who glanced at my business card and laughed when I introduced myself. It was not a laugh of derision, but a chuckle of delight. When I asked her what she found so entertaining, she told me she had a master's degree in graphic design and her experience with most consultants was that their logos were not memorable. They did not project a polished, professional image. This logo, however, was in her opinion a very strong business-to-business communications platform.

Summary

As I charted the path for writing this book – to describe the development of the Building Bridges to the Future® model – I felt that the personal background I have included in this chapter is important. You might ask, "Why?"

Building a consulting business requires a specific set of action strategies driven by a brand promise that is defined by the brand identity. That brand promise and brand identity is tied to the talents, skills and values of the founder or principals. These talents, skills and values are honed by life experiences and life choices.

Chapter Two continues on this path. My business and the business model described in this book are grounded in the life experiences described in these first two chapters.

A Corporate Eye Doctor

"There are two kinds of people in the world:
Simplicators and complifiers."

– Mel Nelson

An important part of this book is about the experiences and individuals who along the way helped me develop my talents and abilities. That's the focus of this chapter.

Years ago, one of my good friends who owned a marketing agency told me of a mentor who counseled him: "There are two kinds of people in the world: simplifiers and complicaters. Our job is to be simplifiers." I've never forgotten that, and I've parsed it to:

"There are two kinds of people in the world:
Simplicators and complifiers."

My job is to combine the ideas of my clients' teams into a synthesis of simplicity. Their words. Their ideas. Brought into perfect focus. Leonardo da Vinci said it this way ... "Simplicity is the ultimate sophistication."

But before I can help them see clearly, I must see clearly myself. I've known many consultants who cannot do for themselves what they profess to excel at with clients – focus. My pastor put it well: "If there is mist in the pulpit, there is fog in the pews."

Practicing What I Preach / Walking the Talk / Personal Focus

In a day and age when we are bombarded continually with messages, it is a challenge for our message to cut through the clutter of an over-communicated society and solidly connect with clients. So the idea of developing a sharply-honed business focus for consultants is absolutely critical.

In developing a focus for Executive Management Systems, I chose to leverage the power of networking. One of my networks sponsored a conference in the fall of 2004. The keynote speaker was himself a consultant who advises consultants to develop an "audio logo" which will explain their business concisely and clearly to others. Out of this simple exercise, steeped in a deep knowledge of who I was and a keen awareness of what I was doing in my business, I developed a statement of focus that has worked very well for me.

When people ask me what I do, I do not tell them I am an executive consultant. As a conversation opener, that is the kiss of death. Instead, I tell them, *"I'm a corporate eye doctor* ... [Pause for effect] ... *I help business owners, executives and boards bring their vision into focus."*

Less is more. A creative, simple statement like this usually results in a more extended conversation. By having a sharp focus and a simple, concise statement, we create the opportunity to pique others' curiosity and let them ask questions.

The more extended conversation which usually follows gives me an opportunity to discuss the concept of *"Building Bridges to the Future® ... Developing business strategy in a team setting."*

In the last chapter, I mentioned Charles Swindoll's book *Living Above the Level of Mediocrity*. The basic point of this book is that we were not created to grovel in mediocrity, but to soar ... live life with vision ... see what most people miss ... let that vision guide our choices and actions.

"The eagle's retina has eight times more visual cells per cubic centimeter than the human eye. This gives the eagle astounding visual capabilities. Flying at an altitude of 600 feet, an eagle can spot an object the size of a dime in the grass below. A three-inch fish can be seen jumping in a lake at a distance of five miles."[6]

Effective leaders see what others miss. One important way leaders inspire, motivate, and give direction to an organization is through their shared vision of the organization's future. Effective strategic thinking is critical in developing this vision. A leadership team's ability to develop this keen, positive, motivational view of the future is of vital importance. The successful leader will see what others have seen, but think what no one else has thought.

To develop focused strategy for clients, a consultant must first have a very sharply-defined professional focus. But equally essential are well-polished and comprehensive communication skills, coupled with effective leadership as a facilitator.

Communication

The most fundamental of skills required of a consultant is a full suite of communication talent – the ability to listen, the ability to speak, the ability to write, the ability to engage in meaningful, client-directed conversation.

To flesh out the metaphor of the corporate eye doctor, let me spell out my expectations whenever I'm in need of medical attention. I'm opinionated when it comes to selecting those with

---

[6] Charles R. Swindoll, *Living Above the Level of Mediocrity* (Waco, Texas: Word Books Publisher, 1987) p. 80.

whom I choose to work. I have very specific things in mind and look for these qualities in physicians:

- Professionals who communicate well:
    - Who present information in the context of the big picture, and flesh it out with details as necessary
    - Who listen as well as they speak
    - Who engage in conversation
- Professionals who respect the intelligence of the patient, and are not insulated within a bubble of professional hubris
- Professionals who respect my self-knowledge
- Professionals who want to build a relationship with me to better serve my medical needs, who are gifted individuals who build on the foundation of a personal relationship with me as a patient, a firsthand knowledge of me as an individual
- Professionals who are very skilled technically in their area of specialization
- Professionals who are proactive, anticipating problems while they are still on the horizon

In the day of increasing specialization in medicine, what the profession is sorely lacking is generalists – those who can see the big picture and relate to our needs in the context of our overall well-being. In the care of our aging parents, my wife and I have personally experienced this challenge, and we've had to be very proactive in ensuring that the overall context of medical treatment is always in focus. We know, as we age we will also have to take a very proactive role in our own medical care.

This need for generalists, big-picture thinkers, is a clear need in consulting.

Speaking

My interest in speech was well-developed in my early teen years. The first formal speech I gave was in my ninth-grade English class. My chosen topic of interest was the Zero Gradient Synchrotron at the Argonne National Laboratory, a 12.5 billion electron volt (BeV) particle accelerator under construction and slated for operation in August 1963. I was totally enamored of the topic – high energy physics research – and my speech ran a half hour. It was a real yawner and put people into either an agitated state of frustration or a lethargic state of boredom.

I was not going to let that start keep me from strengthening my speaking ability, however, and I persevered. Eighteen years later, I spoke at the Institute of Electrical and Electronic Engineers Power Engineering Conference in Vancouver, B.C. Unbeknownst to me, one of those in the audience was an executive from Northern States Power Company. He felt that my presentation stood head and shoulders above the others at that conference, and within a couple of weeks, nominated me for the prestigious Nikola Tesla award, given by the Westinghouse Electric Corporation for meritorious service to the energy industry.

As a professional, I've always enjoyed dissecting complex subjects, boiling the ideas down to the basics, and then communicating them simply to others.

Writing

Communication begins with language, and I was blessed with a mother who was intelligent and understood language – in fact four of them: Norwegian, Latin, French, and English. She was an excellent speller and energetically played the word game "Scrabble" into her eighties. A Registered Nurse, she understood the importance of language and communication ... and that excellence in communication started with good written language skills.

My mother's impact on my language skills was indelible. I chuckle as I think of one of my mentors who offered, "Mel, you use too many Latinized words in your speaking and writing. You should use simpler words ..." He strengthened his mentoring by giving me a copy of the book, *How to Write, Speak and Think More Effectively* by Rudolph Flesch, and I'm grateful for his counsel, and his willingness to invest in my life.

Listening

In my work with business leaders, developing the leadership skill of listening has been a fascinating experience. Capturing, paraphrasing and restating others' points of view – in their language – lead to powerful communication. The following quotes are insights offered by participants in these sessions:

"Great communicators make great leaders ... and listening is 75% of communication."

"Good listeners are often under-appreciated in some business cultures."

"Effective leadership builds on understanding others ... How can leaders understand without thoughtful listening?"

"Certainly leaders cannot know it all ... Listening is critical to understanding and gaining insight."

John Drakeford, in his book *The Awesome Power of the Listening Ear,* calls listening "a forgotten factor in leadership." He quotes the famous artist Norman Rockwell who was commissioned to paint President Eisenhower's portrait:

"'The general and I didn't discuss politics or the campaign. Mostly, we talked about painting and fishing. But what I remember most about the hour and a half I spent with him was the way he gave me all his attention. He was listening to me and talking to me, just as if he hadn't a care in the world, hadn't been through the trials of a political convention, wasn't on the brink of a presidential campaign."[7]

Drakeford also noted the listening skills of President Johnson:

"Although he once taught speech in Texas schools, even his most enthusiastic admirers would not venture to call President Johnson a great orator. His strength apparently lies in his personal face-to-face encounters with members of Congress. One of his subordinates describes the way in which the President functions: 'Does he listen? He listens so hard it's deafening.' Learning to listen, he acquired potent leadership skills."[8]

It is important to expand the listening process by seeing four different aspects of listening:

"Noticing what has not been said is an important part of active listening. The active listener is a skillful questioner, using the techniques of reflecting, probing, supporting, and advising to encourage the other party to extend the conversation and clarify the message."[9]

---

[7] Norman Rockwell, "My Adventures As an Illustrator," ed. T. Rockwell, *Saturday Evening Post,* CCXXXIX (September 24, 1966) p. 24.
[8] John Drakeford, *The Awesome Power of the Listening Ear* (Waco, Texas: Word Books, 1967), p. 91.
[9] *Essential Skills of Communicating* (Omaha, NE: Vital Learning, 2010) . p. 78.

Active Listening

Reflecting
Verify and Clarify

Probing
Ask Clarifying Questions

Supporting
Express Feelings

Advising
Provide Facts

© Copyright 2010 Vital Learning Corporation. Used with permission.

Self-Awareness / Personal Listening Style

One of the key premises driving my work in leadership development is the value of self-awareness and other-awareness. In helping clients achieve focus, a keen personal awareness of our individual listening style *vis-à-vis* a universal model of listening styles is very useful.

One of the "systems" I use in my consulting practice is the Personal Listening Profile®, a powerful tool to understand our listening style in the context of the universe of human approaches to listening. This construct embraces five approaches to listening, which in turn define 15 styles of listening. Our individual style is defined by one or more predominant approach(es) to listening.

For me personally, my listening style is analytical, which is a combination of the comprehensive and evaluative approaches. As such, my personal focus in listening is to understand and evaluate information. This listening style brings these qualities to the table[10]:

- **Focus**
    - o Finding the underlying meaning
    - o Organizing ideas
- **Tendencies**
    - o Immediately organizing information to make sense
    - o Listening for the big picture
    - o Identifying main ideas
    - o Looking for the "message behind the message"
    - o Understanding the core relationships among ideas
    - o Drawing even deeper conclusions from those ideas
    - o Thinking conceptually about the information I'm receiving
    - o Easily elaborating on the main ideas
    - o Searching for facts to support the main message
    - o Understanding the rationale used to develop an argument
    - o Readily asking questions to clarify speaker's message
- **Strengths**
    - o Analyzing information in a deep and critical fashion
    - o Taking more away from a conversation than simple facts and details
    - o Identifying the unspoken, deeper message
    - o Elaborating on ideas and recognizing their implications
    - o Critically evaluating the quality of information as it is presented
    - o Drawing conclusions and making decisions that are well thought out

---

[10] Personal Listening Profile®, Inscape Publishing. Used with permission.

- **Summary**
  - My style is purposeful
  - I'm listening to make an informed and accurate decision
  - It's important that my conclusions are accurate and well-anchored in fact

This style has served me well. Because of the elaborate processing of the information, long-lasting memory is a result.

Bats Listen Very Well

I saw my first bat when I was eight. Ever since I was in junior high, I've had a deep fascination with bats' ability to listen. It's a key defining quality of who and what they are. Bats emit a varied series of high frequency chirps that are frequency modulated and enable them to do remarkable things. Their ultrasound chirps are above the frequencies we hear. We can honestly and accurately say that we are not on their wavelength.

Bats can fly very precisely and closely to objects. They can do a 90° wingover to fly through bars that are more closely spaced than their wing span. They can use their advanced sonar capabilities to detect, identify, pursue, and feast on insect prey. When closing in on prey, their chirp pulse rate goes up significantly for accuracy in their pursuit. Because of their highly-refined sonar navigation capabilities, the U.S. Navy studies bats.

Bats live or die on their ability to listen to reflected sounds and intelligently process the information received. Business leaders and consultants who follow their example will do well.

Identifying Individual Perspectives

When listening to the same conversation, how many people listen to it from the same perspective? A perfectly-cut diamond has 57 facets. It is not only a work of art and a product of the wonders of nature – it is a masterpiece of craftsmanship. No other object in creation can sparkle and reflect light as does a diamond with perfect color, clarity, and cut.

I often use the example of the diamond in my leadership development sessions on listening by asking people to imagine a large model of a diamond in my hand. As I hold this imagined model up to the group, with its fifty-seven different sides, I ask the question, "How many of you now see this diamond from exactly the same perspective?" The answer I've never failed to get is, "None of us."

Thus it is with communication and conversation. The only way we can move our perception and understanding to a common ground is by active listening and the skillful use of questions.

Another key insight from the example of the diamond is what we miss by not paying close attention to detail, a lack of awareness. A follow up question I like to ask is, "Viewed from above and below, what images do you see in a perfectly cut diamond?" I have never had an audience yet with the right answer. From above, we see an "arrows" pattern; from below we see a "hearts" pattern. This ties in very nicely with the central idea that diamonds and Cupid go hand-in-hand.

The Role of Strategic Questions

Strategic questions combined with active listening are a valuable communications strategy. One of my mentors told me early in my career, *"Mel, you should make fewer assertions and ask more questions."* Good advice. It was advice that I took.

Questions prime the listening pump. They are a powerful and critical communications tool. They go hand-in-hand with good listening skills. They are essential to drawing out a client's best thinking. They force me to practice deferred judgment, to stay in the present moment and not race ahead … to my next thought.

Interactive listening – done well – includes asking questions to verify and clarify what has been said. Clarifying questions probe deeper for better understanding. Quantity breeds quality. Lots of questions generate a lot of insights. The net sum of these insights gives valuable cues to direction-setting.

Facilitation as Leadership

Merriam-Webster defines facilitator as *"one that helps to bring about an outcome … by providing indirect or unobtrusive assistance, guidance, or supervision."* The word "facilitator" is little bit of a lame word and is too often coupled with low expectations. Let me give you an example.

A lame definition of facilitation relegates this important role to low expectations. One of the books I have on my shelf sets forth practical wisdom for effective groups. When I facilitate, I don't want an effective group, I want a team that is going to play ball and win! To give you an idea of how lame the defined role of facilitator is in this 293-page book, the index points out that the word "leadership" first appears on page 250!

In actuality, facilitation done well is a very unique form of leadership. It's a sophisticated way of bringing out the best in others. It's a leadership role to chart the journey of self-discovery for a team. An effective facilitator will ultimately work himself / herself out of a job, because he / she has had a transformational impact on the dynamic of the leadership team.

Facilitation is a role of leading process, not content. Let's explore the area of team innovation as an example.

Years ago, I learned the ABCs of brainstorming: "A – *all ideas are accepted;* B – *borrowing is encouraged;* C – *criticism is not allowed."* In the heavily left-brain, logical, analytical world of business, it's tough to take the time to be creative. In fact, I've heard it said that it's tough to graduate from a university and have any right-brained creativity left. Analyticals (engineers, accountants, attorneys, doctors, bankers – to name a few) are quick to identify why something will not work, rather than playfully exploring how something could work.

The game in too many team settings is a version of Yosemite Sam's antics. You have your six-shooter on your hip in a well-oiled holster, ready to clear leather the instant someone floats a new idea. The object of the game is to empty your six-gun before the idea lands on the table, and blow the idea full of holes. With a look of satisfaction, you blow the smoke from the barrel, re-holster your six-shooter, and rhetorically, your look of smug satisfaction begs the other team members' approval: *"What did you think of that excellent marksmanship?"*

A key leadership role in facilitation is to have members of the team check their guns at the door, and deal firmly and swiftly with any Yosemite Sam wannabes who will shoot down innovation in a heartbeat. One of the in-depth executive talent assessments I use specifically identifies those who cannot create new ideas, but can tell you what is wrong with an idea. This skill is very useful in some leadership positions, but is an absolute killer in others ... and it's a proven killer of innovation if it is the first step a team uses in the process.

Let's look more closely at facilitator process leadership for team innovation. It has everything to do with creating an atmosphere for the free exchange of ideas, rather than creating those ideas themselves. The ideas come from the team and it is the facilitator's role to lead the team through the process of

1. Exploration for ideas,
2. A playful stage of developing possibilities,
3. Ranking and refining options as most workable and likely to succeed, and
4. Implementation / execution.

Roger von Oech (*A Kick in the Seat of the Pants*) has defined these four stages as: Explorer, Artist, Judge and Warrior.[11] Inscape Publishing has defined these four stages as Creator, Advancer, Refiner and Executor. Individuals have a tendency to naturally function in one of these roles. There is a fifth role of Flexer, where an individual can move freely to any of the four roles.[12]

I have found it very helpful to identify the innovation culture of a team. It is a very useful diagnostic as a predictor of team performance in innovation. In one situation, I split a leadership team of 15 into three groups of five, and assigned individuals to each group based on achieving a balance in each group of the five roles. Why three groups? Fifteen was too large a group for the innovation process, and with three groups, we could "cycle" our development of strategy through several steps, adding clarity and value along the way. Why five in a group? It's an ideal-sized group, especially for innovation when all roles are represented in the group. With this client, it was a very productive approach because –

---

[11] Roger Von, Oech, *A Kick in the Seat of the Pants: Using Your Explorer, Artist, Judge, & Warrior to Be More Creative* (New York: Perennial Library, 1986).
[12] *Team Dimensions Profile 2.0 Group Report* (Inscape Publishing, 2005) p. 3.

through assessment – I knew the natural roles of each in the team and the overall team innovation culture.

When done well, effective facilitation is viewed as magic. It truly is a unique and sophisticated leadership role.

My Mentors

Mentoring is very helpful for *"individuals to acquire skills, open doors, increase confidence, widen perspectives, avoid many errors, and otherwise enhance their careers and lives."*[13] This chapter would not be complete without mention of the mentors who have had a major impact on who I am and what I do.

At the top of the list are my mother and father. My mother gave me a passion for the pursuit of learning and acquisition of knowledge. She built my confidence in my ability to learn. She created a learning environment with high yet attainable expectations. My father was a man of integrity, well-grounded in God's Truth. He was very effective at building personal relationships. He knew how to laugh.

I learned much from many I worked with in the electric power industry over the years. Andy Freeman, Lyle Lund, Lloyd Hillier, Bill Juhnke, to name a few. As an avid student of military history, I've learned much from the military heroes who have nobly served our country and whose gripping firsthand accounts of their military service inspire, motivate and serve as poignant illustrations of critical leadership and life principles.

---

[13] L. Phillips-Jones, *The New Mentors & Protégés* (Grass Valley, CA: Coalition of Counseling Centers 1997) p. 9.

I've had many close, mentoring friendships in the consulting field. John Butler was one who rose to the top in my experience, and I speak to that in Chapter Five.

One other leader I consider my mentor – although I've never talked to him personally – is Chuck Swindoll. His prolific writing and speaking career as a bible teacher has had a continual impact on my life over the last thirty years. His life experiences, perspective, and wisdom have had particular relevance to my work in the business world over the last thirty years. Some of that impact will be clear as you read this book.

Surprisingly, my children have also been mentors to me. The investment my wife and I have made in their lives has paid a healthy return with the acquired wisdom they've shared with me, the mutual respect we enjoy, the conversation we share and the sense of community we have built. Their walk of faith as they chart their path to the future has been inspiring and encouraging.

Relational Elements of Mentoring

In my personal research on executive coaching, I came across a dissertation by Manda H. Rosser that makes a fundamental statement on the impact of mentors. It is the strength of the personal relationship that makes the difference between success and failure in mentoring. The successful mentoring I've received was seminal in the development of the Building Bridges to the Future® model and the centrality of how critical solid relationships are in leadership performance. (I'll go into depth on that in Chapter Five.)

In her dissertation, Rosser notes the work of K.E. Kram[14]: In the most effective mentoring relationships, personal development is enabled by the emergence and strengthening of interpersonal connections between the mentor and protégé that foster mutual trust and increase intimacy.

Rosser goes a significant step further in her research by identifying the significant attributes, values, and actions at the core of a successful mentoring relationship[15]:

Attributes	Values	Actions
Admiration	Trust	Support and encouragement
Pride	Honesty	Appreciation
Confidence (Believed in me)	Respect	Personal interest or connection
Not letting them down (Obligation)	Caring	Attention (Time)
Inspiration and Aspiration	Open Communication	Listening (Communicated)

A most conclusive finding from Rosser's research was "The most significant insight provided by the CEOs was the importance that the relational elements played in their development."

---

[14] K.E Kram, "Phases of the Mentor Relationship," *Academy of Management Journal,* 26 (1983) pp. 608-625.
[15] Manda K. Rosser, "Chief Executive Officers: Their Mentoring Relationships," Ph.D. dissertation, Texas A&M University (December 2004) p. 128, Table 6.

Mentors After 50

An interesting phenomenon hit me after nearly three decades in the workforce. All of a sudden, I was 50 ... my mentors were gone, retired. I'd always valued learning from others. To whom now could I look for mentoring? Should I now become a mentor? Turns out I had been for many years. ... As I looked back on comments offered by many younger colleagues and co-workers, colleagues ten, twenty or thirty years younger than me, I was encouraged. These three comments were typical:

"I've never known anyone who could simplify and explain things like you ..."

"You had a big impact on me and my career. I learned a lot from you in those years we worked together."

"Your positive energy and continual, multi-dimensional, deliberate approach to life is why you are such an excellent role model."

But there was no getting around it. I now had few – if any – to mentor me. I thought it was over for me as a mentee ... but I was wrong. I've found many who are ten or twenty years further along in life than I who have valuable life-lessons from which I can learn. Among my "senior statesmen" mentors are Dr. Allan Hedberg, George Beaumont, Bud Cummings, and Dr. Dave Mefford.

Summary

This chapter is an important part of this book – the experiences and individuals who along the way helped me develop my talents, abilities, and business mindset. Personal focus. Communication. Speaking. Active listening. Facilitation as leadership. Mentoring.

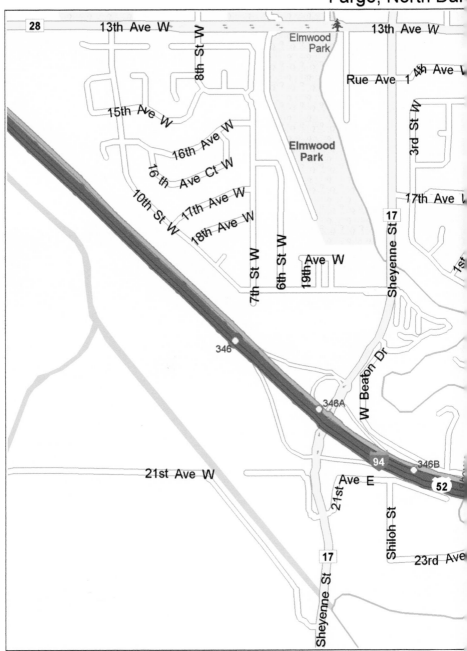

Fargo, North Dak

ota, United States   1721 Princeton Lane

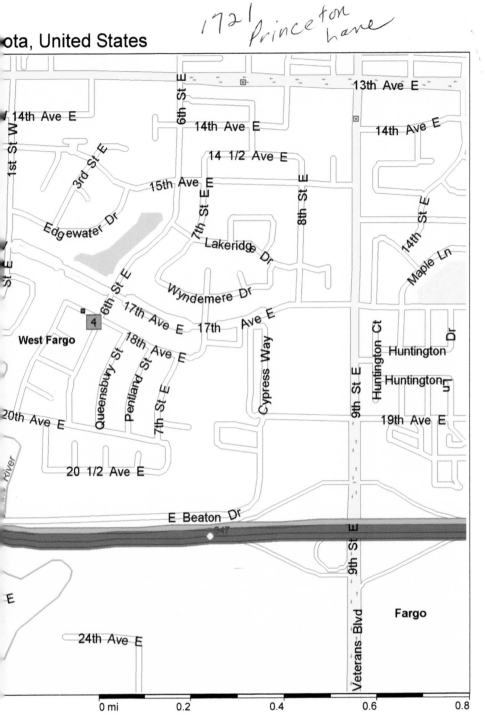

All of the mentoring relationships I've mentioned above – with the exception of my mother and father – have been informal, yet transformational, and have been characterized by the qualities so clearly captured in the table above. These mentors have helped me to achieve greater things than I could have without their influence.

There is one more category of mentors who have shaped my thinking but will go unnamed. These mentors were examples of what *not* to do, how *not* to treat people, how *not* to approach a situation. I owe a debt to these mentors as well, for their significant impact on the choices I make daily in how I lead and treat others.

In the next chapter, we'll discuss how bridges are linked to the process of envisioning the future.

Chapter Three

Bridges –
A Path to the Future

"The great successful men [and women] of the world have used their imagination ... They think ahead and create their mental picture, and then go to work materializing that picture in all its details, filling in here, adding a little there altering this a bit and that a bit, but steadily building – steadily building."

- Robert Collier

"We are told never to cross a bridge until we come to it, but this world is owned by men and women who have 'crossed bridges' in their imagination far ahead of the crowd."

- Speakers Library

Have you ever heard someone say, "I'll cross that bridge when I come to it?" Have you ever considered how limiting that mindset is as a life strategy or as a business strategy?

The present is driven by those who anticipated today while it was still in the future ... when in their minds tomorrow was today.

The strategic heartbeat of Executive Management Systems, Inc. is "Building Bridges to the Future®." This type of bridge-building requires focused business strategy and solid teamwork, starting at the executive level. It also involves change ... building bridges where none existed before ... or reconstructing bridges where the infrastructure is aged and failing, and may be in danger of imminent collapse.

Bridges As Mind Travel

Bridges enable us to go where we've never gone before. In this context, bridges are best understood as a transition from where we are to where we want to go ... they are a means of mind travel from the present to the future.

Bridges to the future begin as bridges in the mind. It is here where obstacle-conquering travel begins. And it is with a leader and the leadership team that a bridge to the future is launched.

As I reflect on bridge-building, two key insights strike me:
1. Although many may initially grasp the basic idea – "Build a bridge here to overcome this obstacle" – there are very few who can turn the vision into reality; and
2. Every major bridge ever constructed in the world was first travelled in the mind of the creator, long before any real traffic actually crossed the bridge.

Winston Churchill touched on mind-travel when he said: *"The only limits are, as always, those of vision."* There is a lot to gain from a purposeful reflection on the psyche of bridge builders as men of vision.

Vision with Precision

As men of vision, bridge builders' view of the future – their bridge vision – has to be one of precision. The Mackinac Bridge took four construction seasons, four years, to build, 1954 to 1957. *The survey effort that brought crystal clarity to the Mackinac Bridge vision, to ensure that the bridge achieved its purpose, was an effort which required two years!*

> "The total surveying job required two full seasons. Before it had ended, the two peninsulas of Michigan had been linked by the precise triangulation and levels of surveyors for the first time in history."[16]

But there is yet one more footnote to "vision with precision." When it was learned that the surveyed locations for the structures placed some on risky geologic features, before construction began the entire bridge was relocated thirty feet north. This could be done with no additional survey work because of the precision of the first survey. Each of the thirty-four bridge piers were moved thirty feet north on their records.[17]

The Psyche of Bridge-Builders

The best bridge builders are talented in multiple dimensions, in a variety of disciplines. In addition, they possess numerous personal skills and qualities. They are courageous, creative, patient, yet results-oriented ... artistic, yet realistic ... and dreamers, yet pragmatists. They are able to engage others in noble pursuits. Their knowledge and practice spans many disciplines – science, engineering, finance, and aesthetics. They are leaders, able to motivate others to take on tough challenges and persist in the face of significant odds.

Their feet are grounded in reality. Yet they are able to *see what others have seen and think what no one has thought.* They have a great deal of in-depth, first-hand life experience and a wealth of insight. These are important tools of the bridge-builder.

---

[16] David B. Steinman and John T. Nevill, *Miracle Bridge at Mackinac* (Grand Rapids: Wm. B. Eerdmans Publishing Co., 1957), p. 53.
[17] Ibid., pp. 68-69.

One of the significant qualities of a bridge builder's psyche is confidence. There are two kinds of confidence – confidence in the laws of physics and personal confidence in their own talents and skills.

The visionary designer and builder of the Mackinac Bridge, David B. Steinman, possessed this confidence:

> *"Often called the world's foremost bridge designer and engineer, Dr. Steinman and his associates designed more than 400 bridges on five continents. He regarded the Mackinac Bridge linking Michigan's two peninsulas as his 'crowning achievement' ... Completed in 1957, the bridge ... exemplifies Steinman's talent for combining beauty in design with engineering utility and durability. With a critical wind velocity of infinity, it represents an aerodynamic stability never before attained in suspension bridge design ..."*[18]

Dr. Steinman had 48 years of professional experience, perspective, insight, and discernment when construction of the bridge began in 1954. This parallels the comment of General Fred Franks, cited in the last chapter, on the necessity for experience and ever-increasing scopes of responsibility for military leaders. Years of seasoned experience are a valuable force to shape the mindset and psyche of a bridge builder: confidence, perseverance and personal accountability.

---

[18] Michigan Transportation Hall of Honor – David B. Steinman (1887-1961)
<http://www.michigan.gov/mdot/0,1607,7-151-9620_11154_41535-126386--,00.html > (21 June 2008)

Confidence in the Laws of Physics

There are fundamental laws of physics which must be understood and addressed to develop an effective design for a bridge. To be successful, a bridge builder must have confidence that these laws of physics apply to bridge design and construction – for better or for worse; and that all applicable laws of physics have been addressed in the bridge design.

The bridge is a combination of numerous individual components and systems. Each system is interlocked to form the whole. The final outcome is dependent on the smoothly integrated components coming together as a whole ... each designed to respect the laws of physics which spell success ... or failure.

On a recent trip to Alaska, my wife and I had a chance to tour a gold mine and pan for gold. To be successful, we had to have absolute confidence in the physics of the process:

- Gravity works; and
- Gold is heavier than sand and gravel.

A small amount of gold ore was placed in the miner's pan. We added water and with a continual and gentle swirling motion, we let the water gradually spill out of the pan and carry away the gravel and fine sand. The gold – still hidden to our eyes – gradually settled to the bottom of the pan. We patiently swirled the water-ore mixture, all the while letting the sand and gravel gradually spill over the edge of the pan. It required patience, a deliberate, steady process, and confidence in physics (gravity) doing its work as we helped it along.

Without patience, and the gradual, gentle action of the swirling water assisting gravity, the gold is dumped with the sand and gravel. Without confidence in the laws of physics, you'll give up. It is critical to gradually let the gold settle as the gentle swirling motion lets the water wash away the waste. It is quite amazing to patiently pan for gold since the reward does not come until the very end. It is only after the sand and gravel has been gently and gradually washed away that the gold emerges. I remember the exhilaration we felt when patience, process and solid confidence in the laws of physics paid off – gold is heavier than rocks or sand; and gravity works.

Personal Confidence

To be successful, a bridge builder must not only have confidence in the laws of physics. One of the significant qualities of a bridge builder's psyche is personal confidence. This personal confidence is not hubris. It is confidence in the model he used for his bridge design. The overall bridge model is comprised of the numerous individual systems that together define the overall bridge structure. Each of these components has been designed with the laws of physics carefully considered.

Each component and system is interlocked with the others to form the whole. The final outcome is dependent on the smoothly integrated components coming together as a whole ... each designed to respect the laws of physics, which spell success ... or failure.

I was reminded of the need for personal confidence in an unusual way during a recent elk hunting trip. Three of us – my oldest son Joel, my brother-in-law Brent, and I – went on horseback into the interior of the Bob Marshall Wilderness Area in Montana. Our confidence had to be uniquely interwoven in all that we did – confidence in our physical capabilities, our hunting skills, our shooting skills, our horsemanship, our stamina, our perseverance, and our guides' abilities.

Nowhere was our confidence more necessary than in our horses. We had a good chance to build our confidence in riding. The ride in was 28 miles. But a forest fire added a detour that took our ride in to 43 miles, extending it from a planned eight hours to 15 hours. The ride out was also extended – to 32 miles – but we made that ride out in just over eight hours. We rode 200 miles during that nine-day hunt.

We entrusted our lives every day to those horses and their ability to navigate narrow trails on steep slopes – at times in the dark. I remember mentally calculating the incline of the slopes we were crossing ... 45°, 60°, 70°, 70°+ ... to where the right or left side was sheer, with a drop of hundreds of feet to a thousand or more. My brother-in-law was with us on the hunt, grew up with horses and has a dozen today. During the hunt, he often said, "I could not do this with my horses."

We could never have done that hunt without absolute confidence in our horses. So, too, must executive consultants have absolute confidence in the models they use to develop solutions for their clients.

Perseverance

In completing the Mackinac Bridge project, David Steinman also possessed the perseverance necessary for a project which had substantial political and financial hurdles to overcome.

Steinman talks about the active opposition to the bridge, the political turmoil, the unfounded stories about the unstable geology in the straits, a state highway department and commissioner who were against the project, a legislature which not only would not commit funds for the bridge, but imposed a tight, unnecessary deadline on the bond issue to build the bridge. The short poem introducing the struggles speaks to this:

Generations dreamed the crossing;
Doubters shook their heads in scorn.
Brave men vowed that they would build it –
From their faith a bridge was born.[19]

Personal Accountability / Oversight

Going back to the Montana elk hunt, in addition to having the necessary confidence in the horses' abilities, we had to assert our control over the horses. We had to take the personal accountability to give oversight to the best efforts of our steeds.

One of the tricks each day, as we saddled up a fresh horse, was to take charge of the horse early in the day, as soon as we mounted up. This assertion of the rider lets the horse know who is in control. Ultimately, it is the rider of the horse who is responsible for the outcome of the ride, not the horse. This is a very important principle.

We rode through a lot of timber on that hunt. Often, the horse would choose a path that gave him clearance from the branches, but not the rider. Time for rider accountability. Don't blame the horse for your lack of assertive control of the horse.

Success in bridge design is a direct outcome of the bridge designer's personal discipline and attention to the model, ensuring that it functions totally within the laws of physics. As executive consultants, we must also be in charge of ourselves, and the process at each step along the way. We must steer the model with our experience and acquired judgment.

---

[19]Op. cit., Steinman, p. 22.

Bridge Failure

Bridges are taken for granted. We often cross them without thinking about how we are entrusting our lives to them. Bridges don't last forever. They require continual inspection, maintenance and vigilance.

Perhaps one of the most poignant illustrations of how we take bridges for granted was forcibly brought to the nation's attention when an I-35W bridge in the Twin Cities spanning the Mississippi River failed:

> *"On Aug. 1, 2007, under stress from 287 tons of construction material and rush-hour traffic, the bridge's center span shuddered, then collapsed, dragging other spans into the river. Thirteen people were killed, and 145 were injured … The bridge, which opened in 1967, was called fracture critical. That meant a failure of any number of structural elements would bring down the entire bridge."*[20]

The National Transportation Safety Board on November 14, 2008 completed a two-day hearing of its one-year probe of the bridge failure:[21]

> "The bridge collapse started at an area of inferior steel elements known as gusset plates, federal transportation investigators said Thursday, faulting the original design of a critical element of the bridge that fell into the Mississippi River …
>
> 'This terrible tragedy began some 40 years ago with an inadequate design of a gusset plate or, in this case, a number of gusset plates,' NTSB Chairman Mark Rosenker said …

---

[20] "Bridge Reviews Imperfect," *The Forum*, 15 November 2008.
[21] "Experts: Bridge Policy Better," *The Forum, 14 November* 2008.

Investigators focused their report Thursday on gusset plates half as thick as they should have been and the effect of extra weight from construction materials and equipment on the bridge deck the day of the collapse. They said their investigation ruled out several other theories behind the collapse, including corroded bridge components."

Over a four decade period, 1967 to 2007, the National Transportation Safety Board found:

1. There were 10 examples of design flaws in 80,000 bridges built;
2. Of 24 bridges that collapsed, only five resulted from something other than a collision with the bridge.

Fortunately, bridge failure is rare. But it does happen. The same laws of physics which when addressed spell success in bridge design, when ignored spell disaster.

Bridges Are Time Machines

Bridges span obstacles to progress, barriers to time-effective travel. Bridges are therefore time machines. Just like an aircraft travelling at high speed, they enable us to do more with the time we have ... by shortening the time-path to achieving our goals, and minimizing the investment of a critical resource – our time.

The New River Gorge Bridge in West Virginia is 3,030 feet long and for 27 years was the highest vehicular bridge in the world, crossing the river at a height of 876 feet. It cut travel time between two points on opposite sides of the gorge by 98% – from 45 minutes to 45 seconds.[22]

The Mackinac Bridge, the longest suspension bridge in the western hemisphere – 26,372 feet long – cut what was up to a 19-hour wait and ferry crossing during deer season (the busiest time of the year for the Upper Peninsula ferry)[23] to seven minutes.

Bridges provide time-effective pathways to overcome obstacles which impede our future. They enable us to do more with less time and energy invested. When we're time-limited, bridges overcome natural obstacles to success.

According to Webster, "bridge" can be defined as "a means of connection or transition." As time machines, bridges connect us to our future.

Bridges Overcome Obstacles

Bridges not only span barriers to time-effective travel. They span obstacles to progress. Bridges must be understood in the context of the problems they solve, the previously impassable hurdles they eliminate, and the challenges they span.

Bridges are not built by those who look at obstacles as limiting. Bridge builders see obstacles as opportunities to be taken head-on.

Bridges enable "unimpeded movement". Bridges are a badge of civilization ... man conquering the challenges of nature, science, and economics. They require collaboration on an unprecedented scale. They require a long range vision that

---

[22] *New River Gorge Bridge* < http://en.wikipedia.org/wiki/New_River_Gorge_Bridge > (19 July 2008)
[23] *Modern Marvels: The Mackinac Bridge*, 50 min., The History Channel, 2001, DVD.

is shared by many and becomes a driving, unifying force to engage and overcome the many challenges. They are a tribute to the ingenuity of man. They are demanding in design, requiring very rigorous scientific and engineering analysis. They are demanding in the teamwork required to finance, design, build and maintain them.[24]

Bridges often play a significant role in the development of a regional community – business, recreational. Bridges often have a major socio-economic impact. The Romans were known for their bridges, roads, and aqueducts, many of which were so well-engineered and so well-built that they stand today.[25]

A Bridge Can Be a Lifeline[26][27]

One of my favorite stories as a young boy came from a book of my brother's entitled *The Train that Never Came Back*. It illustrates the principle that a bridge can be a lifeline … a communications medium to save lives.

On the evening of July 6, 1881, a violent mid-summer Iowa storm and flash flooding weakened the Honey Creek Bridge. To test the bridge integrity before a midnight passenger train was due to cross it, a crew of four men took a locomotive across the bridge. The bridge partially collapsed, hurling the locomotive and the four men into the raging torrent below. Two survived, clinging to the structure.

---

[24] National Geographic Society, *The Builders* (Washington, DC: The Book Division of the National Geographic Society, 1992) pp. 10-11 paraphrase.
[25] Ibid.
[26] Freeman H. Hubbard, *The Train that Never Came Back* (New York: McGraw-Hill Book Company, Inc., 1952) "The Broken Lantern" pp. 75-86.
[27] "Kate Shelley," Quarry Depot. <http://quarrydepot.com/ks.html> (14 February 2011).

Kate Shelley, a plucky 15-year old Irish immigrant who was the daughter of a railroad man, lived close to the Honey Creek Bridge and heard the crash. Telling her mother she must go to warn others, she took her father's lantern and set out in the raging storm that night.

Crossing the damaged Honey Creek Bridge, she shouted encouragement to the two survivors clinging below, who were later rescued. Once on the other side, she had to run a half mile to get to the Des Moines River Bridge. With rail ties on the bridge two feet apart – big enough to fall through – and with the raging river below, holding a shattered lantern now gone out, she crawled on hands and knees in a race that she had to win – to cross the bridge before the train heading her way. For over two football field lengths – 673 feet – she crawled to reach the depot at Moingona, Iowa and warn the station master of impending disaster.

The Des Moines River Bridge, combined with one very courageous young girl, became a lifeline, a channel of communication to avert disaster for the two hundred passengers and crew on that midnight express.

Formula for Bridges

The bridges of achievement that span the wide chasm, the deep divide between our dreams and reality are a direct outcome of a deliberately planned process. It is a path of discipline. Bridges demand that a formula be satisfied if they are to become reality:

Major Obstacles + Visionary Pragmatists + Collaboration →
Long-term Strategy & Sustainable Results

Without obstacles, we would not have the many examples of creative bridgework throughout the world. Obstacles present a unique opportunity to create stunning examples of human creativity. The longest, tallest and most expensive suspension bridge ever built took a major catastrophe, a public outcry, a robust design, a king's ransom, and over 40 years to create the solution:

> The Akashi Kaikyo Bridge in Japan is the longest, tallest, and most expensive suspension bridge ever built ($4.3 billion), carries 23,000 vehicles a day across the stormy Akashi Straits. The bridge has three spans. The central span is 6,532 feet and the two other sections are each 3,150 feet. With a total length of 12,831 feet, it links the cities Honshu and Awaji. It is designed to withstand winds of up to 180 mph and earthquakes of up to 8.5 on the Richter scale. A primary motivation to build this bridge was to improve the safety of crossing this stormy strait. In 1955, 168 children lost their lives when two ferries sank in a storm. Public outcry led to the design of a bridge – with construction started in 1986, and completion in 1998.[28]

Bridges in Perspective

As I've written this book, I find it helpful to reflect and put the experiential aspect of bridges into perspective.

Bridges travelled in the past often evoke strong memories. For me, these bridges travelled in the past include locations across the world – Lion's Gate, Port Mann, Golden Gate, Mackinac, Ponte del Vechio, Brooklyn Bridge, in addition to numerous other railway trestles, and bridges in North America and Europe.

---

[28] *Akashi-Kaikyō Bridge* < http://en.wikipedia.org/wiki/Akashi_Kaikyo_Bridge > (19 July 2008).

As an executive consultant, I also experience strong memories evoked for me by the bridges of strategy built by executives and their leadership teams. In addition, bridges to the past can evoke strong memories.

Some bridge designers have more vision than others. Some bridges don't last very long ... others survive for centuries. Some bridges succeed immediately. They quickly exceed their design capacity and must be expanded and re-envisioned / re-engineered. Sometimes this gap between capacity and need is driven by a limited vision of the designer, or sometimes by a limited vision of the owner(s). Sometimes the initial bridge design is so limiting, it requires a fresh start.

Once you're on a bridge, it's difficult to get off. To stop ... To turn around ... To jump ... Let's face it, when you move onto a bridge, you're committed. You don't want to get caught on a bridge that is failing.

Crossing bridges can be scary, worrisome, and nerve wracking ... but they enable us to take on the challenge of new frontiers when we reach the other side.

Jumping from bridges is suicidal ... but with a bungee cord or parachute attached, it can be entertaining.

All bridges are not equal. The Chesapeake Bay Bridge & Tunnel was designated "One of Seven Engineering Wonders of the Modern World" in 1965. Not all bridges achieve this level of distinction.

Bridges Outlive Their Creators

It's been my good fortune that whenever I've owned a house, I've always had good neighbors. I recall a conversation I had with one neighbor over twenty-three years ago, about the fence that was on our property line which he had put in ten years previous. "That d--- fence ... I should tear it down," he said one day in frustration. It was a soft wood pole fence with two 10-foot horizontal pieces between each vertical member which sagged with age, yet had a very rustic look and feel to it. The fence pieces had begun to disintegrate with age and the horizontal pieces kept falling out of the holes in the vertical poles.

Unfortunately, my neighbor was diagnosed with an aggressive cancer not long after and soon passed away. I made some minor repairs to the fence. It outlasted its creator by 15 years.

Think about it. Most bridges have a design life of 50+ years. Many bridges last much longer. In most cases, bridges outlive their creators. This reality has caused me to reflect: How well-designed are the bridges you and I are building in this life?

Suspension Bridges – The Metaphor Takes Shape

The Mackinac Bridge is a well-designed bridge that has already outlived its creator by 50 years. It is an excellent visual story board which inspired the development of the Building Bridges to the Future® model.

Suspension bridges are defined by the fact that the bridge span and road deck are "suspended" by cables which are supported by high towers. The cables are solidly anchored at both ends. The towers are firmly connected to massive footings (technically defined as "piers").

We will consider each of these structural components in the next four chapters, in the order in which each is completed in construction:

- The cable anchorages (Chapter Four)
- The towers & footings (Chapter Five)
- The suspension cables (Chapter Six)
- The spans (Chapter Seven)

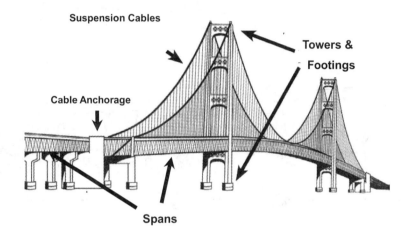

Building Bridges to the Future®

© 2010 Executive Management Systems, Inc.

The illustration on the following pages clearly identifies the elements of a suspension bridge as they apply to the "bridges" business model:

- Cable anchorages = Values+
- Towers / Footings = Relationships+
- Suspension Cables = Leadership+
- Spans / Road Deck = Strategy+

Building Bridges to the Future®

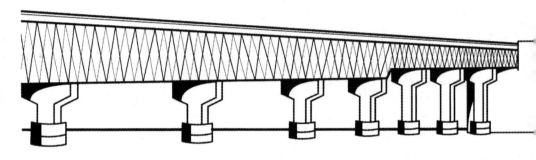

Cable Anchorages

Towers / Footings

Suspension Cables

Spans / Road Deck

Values⁺

Relationships⁺

Leadership⁺

Strategy⁺

Bridges and Business Principles

Suspension bridges can be viewed as a model which serves as a compelling illustration of business systems. They prompt us to think of a bridge as an integrated system which includes critical elements which are not seen and are easily and too often overlooked. Your business is a system ... any weak link weakens the entire system. So much in a bridge is critical.

One link overlooked can cause the entire bridge or business to collapse. You cannot employ linear thinking to solve systems problems in your business.

Bridges imply choices. One choice is to survive where you are ... or aim higher and build a bridge to a better future. Another choice? Once the bridge is built, venture onto it, and boldly cross ... from one state to another. But whatever your choice, be sure that the integrated systems are in place to support your action.

Summary

The key premise of this chapter is that bridges truly are a path to the future.

The bridges that span the gulf of achievement between our dreams and reality are a direct outcome of a planned process. Bridges require time, resources, and champions. Bridges showcase man's ingenuity, creativity, intelligence, expertise and resourcefulness.

With the foundation that has been laid in the first three chapters of this book, the stage is set for a thoughtful, in-depth exploration of the Building Bridges to the Future® metaphor and model. The structural components of a suspension bridge set the stage for the next four chapters.

What makes the Mackinac Bridge succeed is that it is a system of integrated parts. A full 90% of the bridge mass is concrete, the footings that support the superstructure. It is those footings which firmly anchor the bridge on bedrock ... and it is with Piers 17 and 22 – the cable anchorages ... that the development of the metaphor begins: **Values⁺.**

Chapter Four

Cable Anchorages / Values⁺

"As a face is reflected in water, so the heart reflects the real person."

– Solomon

"The high-caliber organization is, after all, merely a reflection of its people."

– Price Pritchett

What is critically important in driving personal and organizational effectiveness that does not meet the eye? What is critically important but is not readily visible? This is a very important question. Behind this question lies a very important principle for business leaders and organizations: "Values run deeper and are far more important to a leader's effectiveness than any other factor."[29]

Mackinac Bridge Stats[30]

Begun in March of 1954 and dedicated in November of 1957, the Mackinac Bridge project was the largest peacetime assembly of construction equipment to that date. With a total structure just over 1,000,000 tons, 900,000 tons is in the substructure, and 100,000 tons is in the superstructure.

There are 33 concrete piers in the water and one on land, a total of 34, which provide the solid footing for the bridge superstructure.

---

[29] Dr. Sid Buzzell, General Editor, *The Leadership Bible: Leadership Principles from God's Word*, (Grand Rapids, MI: Zondervan Publishing House, 1998) p. 635.

[30] *Modern Marvels: The Mackinac Bridge*, 50 min., The History Channel, 2001, DVD.

Pier 17, one of the two cable anchorages, is approximately one mile from shore. It was the starting point for construction of the bridge. It is a 180,000 ton structure. Pier 22, the other cable anchorage, is an identical structure.

In the bridge metaphor, the two cable anchorages correspond to the values of the organization. (In the next chapter, we'll address the tower footings, two more of the thirty-four piers – which in the metaphor represent personal integrity and emotional intelligence.)

What Does Not Meet the Eye?

Of the total tonnage of the Mackinac Bridge, 75% lies beneath the water line. In the bridge metaphor we've been developing, that 75% is in the cable anchorages and footings: organizational values, personal integrity, and emotional intelligence.

Although easily overlooked, the cable anchorages play a major role in bridge integrity. They bear the major portion of the total bridge weight, which is called loading. Although the spans and the main tower/footing structures share in supporting the combined weight of the span superstructure and the bridge traffic, most of this combined weight is ultimately transferred by the suspension cables to the anchorage structures.

This is a fundamental premise in understanding the Building Bridges to the Future® metaphor. Values and personal ethics are the fundamental, bedrock anchors for solid corporate performance. Without them, there is no absolute anchor for leadership performance, no benchmark for corporate performance.

These corporate values should be just as much a corporate anchor as piers 17 and 22 of the Mackinac Bridge, just as definitive and immovable:

"If an organization is to meet the challenges of a changing world, it must be prepared to change everything about itself except [its basic] beliefs as it moves through corporate life.[31]

Values provide a fundamental anchor for not only individuals and organizations, but also for nations. Zhao Xiao is Chairman of Cypress Leadership Institute, and a Professor at the University of Science and Technology in Beijing. "A prominent Chinese economist, Dr. Zhao Xiao was commissioned by his government to study the success of the American economy. He concluded that a moral foundation allowed the economy to flourish, argued that China's economy would benefit from the spread of the Christian faith, and embraced Christianity himself. He continues to be a respected scholar and government advisor, speaking openly about the influence of Christianity on economics."[32]

Values – Central to Who I Am

By observation and having read the previous chapters of this book, you undoubtedly know by now that values are very central to who I am, what I do, and how I perceive the world of business. Values are central in my personal life, my marriage and my family life, and my professional life.

It should come as no surprise that values are a central part, a key component of my business model Building Bridges to the Future®.

---

[31]Thomas J. Watson, *A Business and Its Beliefs*, as quoted by James C. Collins & Jerry I. Porras, *Built to Last: Successful Habits of Visionary Companies* (New York: HarperCollins Publishers, Inc., 2002) p. 81.
[32] " Zhao Xiao." <http://willowcreek.com/events/leadership/2010/speaker_zhao_xiao.asp> (21 Aug. 2010)

Perspective

Bear with me for a minute as I set the stage for the discussion to follow. In my discussion in this chapter on values, I would like to take you with me down these intertwined paths. First, I'd like to set forth some working definitions of the key terms and concepts related to values. Next, I'd like to entertain some perspectives, insights and reflection. I'd also like to explore an example of three driving core values with real meat on the bone. I'd like to tell a couple of stories ... in fact, I'll start with one.

A Story about Values-Driven Behavior

When one of my sons was in eighth grade, he went from doing "A" work in math to failing in three weeks. He had always been an excellent student, so we were quite surprised to learn of his slip in performance. We quickly worked through this bump in the road. He went on to a very successful conclusion of his high school and university education, with a quick entry into a career.

The slide in performance began in early December. We did not become aware of it as parents until late January when he came home with a slip notifying us of this development. The conversation I had with him I recall very clearly:

"Michael, you're very smart. You're a good student. You can do this. I will work with you every night to help you work through this. Here is what we'll do. First, math is hard work. We won't work when you're tired. If you need to get a good night's rest, we'll do it in the morning. Second, in your math problems, I want you to write down every step. Don't crowd it. Write large enough. Make sure you can see each step clearly. Third, check you work. If you find a mistake and have to erase it, make sure it's not smudged so you cannot see each step clearly. Take another sheet of paper if you need to. Paper is cheap."

For the next three weeks, we worked on each math assignment together. We talked through every problem. It was important for him to take the initiative. It was important for me to provide a supportive learning environment. In these three weeks, he pulled it out and was back on his own.

Six weeks after we got the slip giving us notice of his failing work, we had parent-teacher conferences. When I met with his math instructor, she told me Michael had had some problems earlier, but had recovered and was now doing well. I told her, *"Well, I just want to encourage you and let you know the system is working. When we got notice six weeks ago of failing work, here is what we did as parents."* I told the story to her of our work as parents behind the scenes and thanked her for letting us know there was a problem.

She was quite surprised and somewhat shocked, although pleasantly. Her response was on two fronts: *"I'm surprised that a parent would take this amount of time to work with a child; and I'm surprised that a child would take instruction from a parent."* She also added: *"This is remarkable. You should be teaching this course."*

This story has a sequel. Six weeks after the parent-teacher conferences, I relayed this story to the head of the math department in the high school. He said, *"Actually, most students will hit a wall where they have to begin to think abstractly. If they're patient and don't lose hope and don't give up, they'll break through. Unfortunately, many don't. You provided for your son what he needed to break through – encouragement, support, hope, persistence."*

This is a story of values-driven behavior, which illustrates three core values: My wife and I believe that we as parents were responsible overall for the education and training of our family; then as now, we see the family as the fundamental building block in society; and we believe we are accountable as parents, therefore we intend to meet our responsibilities. [When you read Chapter Eight –

"Living Life with Vision" – you will also see how central our values as husband and wife have been in driving our shared vision.]

The point of this story is that deeply held values drove my behavior as a parent. My role as a parent was enhanced by the actions I took because of my values. My son benefited from my values-driven behavior. His teacher was encouraged and amazed.

The broader point is that a critical part of successful parenting is values-driven behavior, and it is imperative that the values driving that behavior be values worth having.

Furthermore, I believe the same to be true in business: A critical component of successful business operations is values-driven behavior, and it is imperative that the values driving that behavior be values worth having.

Interestingly, when my son reviewed my account of this illustration, he said, "I remember that." He also said, "An interesting additional fact you should add is that my teacher had a verse posted by the pencil sharpener, quoting the wisdom of Solomon: 'Train up a child in the way he should go and when he is old, he will not depart from it.'" It struck me that the teacher's behavior was also driven by values we shared in common.

A footnote here is appropriate. As an adult, Michael leads a values-driven life. A little over seven years after the above story took place, my wife and I were six weeks into the major life and career transition I mentioned earlier. On Valentine's Day of 2000, my wife sent a letter to each of our children. Michael's response speaks to his values:

Mom –

Thanks so much for the letter. It was very meaningful to me. I'm so thankful for you and your love for us. It's been quite a ride, this life. I know that you and dad are in a very stretching time, and I continually pray for you. I think God has you where he wants you, and I can't wait to see what will come of this.

Love you, Mom & Dad – Michael

As we went through that difficult time as husband and wife, the return on investment that we had made in the lives of our children, was a wonderful gift to us. This example illustrates a life principle and business principle I believe to be true: Values-driven behavior earns big dividends.

Basic Definitions

Values are not seen, but the behaviors they drive are quite visible. An in-depth discussion of values requires a clear definition of basic concepts at the outset. There are five interrelated concepts and terms begging clear definition and clarification as we explore the cable anchorage in the bridge metaphor: Value, Values, Culture, Beliefs, Organizational / Corporate Culture. Please bear with me as I set the stage for a discussion to follow by setting the plate with some basic definitions.

Value

"Something (as a principle or quality) intrinsically valuable or desirable."[33]

---

[33] "Value," *Dictionary and Thesaurus - Merriam-Webster Online* <http://www.merriam-webster.com/dictionary/value> (29 Apr. 2010).

"A quality that gives something special worth."[34]

"The principles, standards, or qualities which guide human actions."[35]

Note the progression here: desirable, special worth, guide for action.

Values

"In general, important and enduring beliefs or ideals shared by the members of a culture about what is good or desirable and what is not. Values exert major influence on the behavior of an individual and serve as broad guidelines in all situations."[36]

This definition begins to bring culture into the mix and notes that values are powerful drivers of behavior.

Culture

"Broadly, social heritage of a group (organized community or society). It is a pattern of responses discovered, developed, or invented during the group's history of handling problems which arise from interactions among its members, and between them and their environment. These responses are considered the correct way to perceive, feel, think, and act, and are passed on to the new members through immersion and teaching. Culture determines what is acceptable or unacceptable, important or unimportant, right or wrong, workable or unworkable. It encompasses all learned and shared, explicit or tacit, assumptions, beliefs, knowledge,

---

[34] "Value," *Dictionary and Thesaurus - Merriam-Webster Online* <http://www.merriam-webster.com/thesaurus/value> (29 Apr. 2010).
[35] "Value." *Wikipedia - The Free Encyclopedia* <http://en.wikipedia.org/wiki/Value> (29 Apr. 2010).
[36] "Values." *BusinessDictionary.com - Online Business Dictionary*. <http://www.businessdictionary.com/definition/values.html> (29 Apr. 2010).

norms, and values, as well as attitudes, behavior, dress, and language."[37]

Of interest here is the pairing of values and culture as powerful drivers of behavior.

Beliefs

"Assumptions and convictions that are held to be true, by an individual or a group, regarding concepts, events, people, and things." [38]

It is noteworthy to consider the aspect of assumptions – which can be right or wrong. Values "held to be true," but which are actually fallacious and erroneous, set up the organization for misdirected behavior and a great deal of heartache. A fundamental litmus test of any statement of corporate values is what role truth plays in the corporate culture.

Organizational Culture / Corporate Culture

BusinessDictionary.com's definition of organizational culture is helpful. I've broken it up into several pieces:[39]

1. Organizational culture is the "Pervasive, deep, largely subconscious, and tacit code that gives the 'feel' of an organization and determines what is considered right or wrong, important or unimportant, workable or unworkable ... and how it responds to ... unexpected crises, jolts, and sudden change."

---

[37] "Culture." *BusinessDictionary.com - Online Business Dictionary*
<http://www.businessdictionary.com/definition/culture.html> (29 Apr. 2010).
[38] "Beliefs." BusinessDictionary.com - Online Business Dictionary
<http://www.businessdictionary.com/definition/beliefs.html> (29 Apr. 2010).
[39] "Organizational Culture." *BusinessDictionary.com - Online Business Dictionary*
<http://www.businessdictionary.com/definition/organizational-culture.html> (29 Apr. 2010).

2. "All new employees must assimilate this code ('learn the ropes') to know the correct way to behave and what to expect from other employees."

3. "Organizational culture is the sum total of an organization's past and current assumptions, experiences, philosophy, and values that hold it together, and are expressed in its self-image, inner workings, interactions with the outside world, and future expectations. It is based on shared attitudes, beliefs, customs, express or implied contracts, and written and unwritten rules that the organization develops over time and that have worked well enough to be considered valid."

4. "Also called corporate culture, it manifests in

   a. the ways the organization conducts its business, treats its employees, customers, and the wider community,

   b. the extent to which autonomy and freedom is allowed in decision making, developing new ideas, and personal expression,

   c. how power and information flow through its hierarchy, and

   d. the strength of employee commitment towards collective objectives ... Expressed commonly as 'It's how we do things here,' it is unique for every organization and one of the hardest things to change."

This definition points out the fact that culture is created a day at a time. Culture is a net sum of the past behaviors that define the organization's history. These organizational behaviors are the net sum of individual behaviors and history.

This definition also points out that culture can be characterized as "strong" or "weak". When we add another dimension of culture, "healthy" or "dysfunctional", we set the stage for a discussion about strong healthy cultures vis-à-vis strong dysfunctional cultures and the huge impacts each has on an organization – for better or worse.

An Important Leadership Principle

Setting the tone, creating the culture, and living the values by personal example is a primary responsibility of leadership. Weak leadership gets the culture it deserves. Organizations with dysfunctional cultures have, or have had, weak leadership at the top.

I shared that insight recently with a respected leader who was putting together a new organization and was focused on the vision and values which were very important to that organization's success going forward. The clarity of that thought – *"Weak leadership gets the culture it deserves"* – was one of the key factors motivating him to deselect one of the team members. He made a tough call because he saw behaviors which did not line up with the values he wanted for the organization. He did not want to lose the opportunity to set the tone at the top and create the culture he wanted and needed for a success.

He got it right – values are not values unless enforced. Too often, values statements do not embody the present moment. They describe what once was. Or perhaps they describe a desired future state. Ideally, values statements describe reality ... the present moment. Unfortunately, this is often not the case. They are too often fiction.

Values are important. They measure the correctness of our direction. They're like a sailboat keel – they help to keep us on course. They help us to set priorities. The definition of core values is a very important process.

Values & Culture

A serious discussion of values cannot be separated from a discussion of organizational culture. It is helpful to visualize values as the seeds to be planted in a garden ... and to visualize the garden itself as the organizational culture.

The seeds ("values") contain the genetic potential for greatness when planted in the garden. If the garden is not tended well, weeds will choke the produce that is the intended and valued end result. Misdirected, undisciplined, inappropriate, unethical behaviors are the weeds that can choke the intended produce of the organization and ensure that the stated intended values do not see the light of day.

It is not difficult to envision a weedy garden. A weedy organizational culture looks and feels the same way ... and projects the same public image. The high values espoused and often conspicuously posted in offices, hallways, and on the corporate Website are nowhere to be found in the daily activities in a corporate culture suffering an extended core values drought.

Culture is directly palpable. It is more tangible than values. Corporate culture is far more powerful than the corporate slogans so nicely printed and hung on the wall. But real values are held internally, and drive behavior. Values-driven behavior is palpable. Sadly, too many organizations' stated values (slogans) are not aligned with the values-driven behavior that permeates the organization.

The net sum of organizational behaviors shapes the organizational culture, and that organizational culture defines the true values of the organization:

Σ [organizational behaviors] → shapes culture → true values defined

Tom Peters put it this way "... *organizational values and purpose are more defined by what executives do than by what they say ...*"[40]

"Values are clear; they are acted out minute by minute and decade by decade by the top brass; and they are well understood deep in the companies' ranks."[41] Yet, the values at the top are not the only values that drive culture.

If pockets of off-target, counter-culture values are allowed to grow in an organization, those values of those values may eventually become the defining values that shape the organizational culture. Think of these pockets of off-target values as weeds. Unless the garden is tended well, the off-target values choke out the intended produce. The garden that results is not the culture desired.

There is another formula that is important to consider in our discussion of how individuals shape the organizational culture. The net sum of personal ethics defines the ethics of the organization:

Σ [personal ethics] → corporate ethics defined

Price Pritchett describes it this way: *"You carve out the organization's character through your daily choices. You shape its conscience as you exercise your own."*[42]

---

[40] Thomas J. Peters and Robert H. Waterman, Jr., *In Search of Excellence* (New York: Harper & Row, 1982), p. 97.
[41] Op. cit., Peters, pp. 97-98.
[42] Price Pritchett, *The Ethics of Excellence* (Dallas, TX: Pritchett & Associates, 1997) cover.

Charles Reade put it this way: *"Sow a thought, and you reap an act; Sow an act, and you reap a habit; Sow a habit, and you reap a character; Sow a character, and you reap a destiny."*[43]

Behavior at all levels of the organization which falls short of the organization's values must be addressed, regularly and routinely. If this is not done, behavior inconsistent with the intended values chokes the culture like weeds in a garden.

Inappropriate Focus

A provocative thought is this: It is fashionable to focus on corporate culture and ignore corporate ethics and values. Mark J. Pastin put it this way:

> *"Even though organizational ethics and organizational culture are closely related, the obsession with culture does not extend to ethics. Ethics is seen either as an add-on embellishment or as an adjunct to the organization's legal compliance efforts. But the truth is that ethics is the heart of organizational culture. In fact, if ethics is the heart of organizational culture, then the myths, symbols, rituals, ideologies, and customs – the elements of culture on which the organizational culture movement focuses – are the fat around the heart, strangling it and destroying its vitality."*[44]

Pastin also offers a provocative thought in that typically, we tend to think of a strong culture as good. He suggests that weak

---

[43] Charles Read. "Sow a thought." <http://www.quotesdaddy.com/quote/159776/charles-reade/sow-a-thought-and-you-reap-an-act-sow-an-act-and-you> (2 June 2011).

[44] Mark J. Pastin, Ph. D., "No Ethics, No Change," in *Lessons in Cultural Change,* edited by Philip R. Thiebert (Arlington, Virginia: Public Utilities Reports, Inc., 1994) p. 335.

culture, strong ethics is better in that it serves as a catalyst for change in an organization ... and that is a profound insight!

The Culture/Values Gap

When you aggregate enough corporations suffering internally from a core values drought, you wind up with a whole business sector in the economy which becomes values-deprived and ethically depraved. James P. Owen, writing of the Wall Street investment business, three to four years ahead of the Economic Tsunami of 2008, said:

> "In my opinion, something has gone horribly wrong in our business, and our self-preservation depends on fixing it. How can we expect clients to entrust us with their hard-won assets when some of the most venerable, best-known firms in the industry have been tarnished? Wall Street has always operated with a system of self-regulation, but clearly, something in that system is broken ... In fact, if you put together all the ethical rules and guidelines adopted by our firms, associations, and regulatory agencies, you would have enough to sink a small battleship."[45]

This brings us to another thought about cable anchorages, values and culture. Values define the anchorage – its dimension, depth, and breadth. But the anchorage is largely composed of concrete which sets up and hardens. Culture is concrete. As it is allowed to "cure", it hardens. This is what Donald N. Sull had in mind when he wrote, "... the system begins to harden. The fresh thinking that led to a company's initial success is often replaced by a rigid devotion to the status quo."[46] This reinforces what Pastin suggests – referenced

---

[45] James P. Owen and David R. Stoecklein, *Cowboy Ethics: What Wall Street Can Learn from the Code of the West,* (Ketchum, ID: Stoecklein Publishing & Photography, 2005) p. 5.
[46] Donald N. Sull, "Why Good Companies Go Bad," in *Harvard Business Review on Culture and Change,* (Boston: Harvard Business School Publishing, 2002) p. 90.

on the previous page – that weak culture, strong ethics is to be preferred over strong culture in that it serves as a catalyst for change in an organization.

The United States Air Force Memorial

I recently visited the USAF Memorial in Washington, DC, and was impressed with the simplicity and elegance of that memorial.

The impact of the memorial is driven by three components.[47]

Resembling the "bomb burst" contrails performed by the USAF Thunderbirds, three impressive stainless steel spires soar to a height of 270-feet and symbolize the three core values of the Air Force;

Below and to the side of the spires stand four eight-foot tall bronze statues of the Memorial's Honor Guard; and

The base of the Memorial is framed by two 56-foot long, 10-foot high inscription walls of beautifully polished granite, with one wall naming USAF Medal of Honor recipients, and the other wall displaying the Air Force's three core values.

These three Core Values are:

- Integrity First
- Service Before Self
- Excellence in All We Do

Less is more. There are only three value statements. Nine words. Talk about focus.

Porras & Collins spoke to this when they wrote: *"Visionary companies tend to have only a few core values, usually between three and six ... only a few values can be truly core – values so fundamental and deeply held that they will change or be compromised seldom, if ever."*[48]

---

[47] "About the Memorial: Quick Facts.". *United States Air Force Memorial – Air Force Memorial.org* <http://www.airforcememorial.org/memorial/facts.asp> (29 Apr. 2010).
[48] James C. Collins & Jerry I. Porras, *Built to Last: Successful Habits of Visionary Companies* (New York: HarperCollins Publishers, Inc., 2002) p. 74.

In addition to the core values are inspiring quotes from those who have served:

Integrity First

"Integrity: A man's word is his bond." – General Jimmy Doolittle, U.S. Army Air Forces' leader of the Tokyo raid

Service Before Self

"I have been recognized as a hero for ten minutes of action over Vietnam, but I am no more a hero than anyone else who has served their country." – A1C John J. Levitlow, Lowest Ranking Airman Medal of Honor Recipient

Excellence in All We Do

"The future is always decided by those who put their imagination to work, who challenge the unknown, and who are not afraid to risk failure." – General Bernard A. Schriever, Father and Architect of the Air Force Space and Ballistic Missile Programs

There is an important principle behind these quotes: Stories embody the values of the organization and must be told and retold to reinforce the values.

I am including in this chapter on values the in-depth description of the first of three core values of the United States Air Force and the intended behavioral outcomes to be driven by those values. It is well worth a thoughtful read.

CORE VALUES OF THE UNITED STATES AIR FORCE[49]

THE CORE VALUES ARE MUCH MORE THAN MINIMUM STANDARDS. THEY REMIND US WHAT IT TAKES TO GET THE MISSION DONE. THEY INSPIRE US TO DO OUR VERY BEST AT ALL TIMES. THEY ARE THE COMMON BOND AMONG ALL COMRADES IN ARMS, AND THEY ARE THE GLUE THAT UNIFIES THE FORCE AND TIES US TO THE GREAT WARRIORS AND PUBLIC SERVANTS OF THE PAST.

THE FIRST CORE VALUE: INTEGRITY FIRST

- THE AIRMAN IS A PERSON OF INTEGRITY, COURAGE AND CONVICTION.
- INTEGRITY IS A CHARACTER TRAIT. IT IS THE WILLINGNESS TO DO WHAT IS RIGHT EVEN WHEN NO ONE IS LOOKING. IT IS THE MORAL COMPASS, THE INNER VOICE, THE VOICE OF SELF-CONTROL AND THE BASIS FOR THE TRUST IMPERATIVE IN TODAY'S MILITARY.
- INTEGRITY IS THE ABILITY TO HOLD TOGETHER AND PROPERLY REGULATE ALL OF THE ELEMENTS OF A PERSONALITY. A PERSON OF INTEGRITY, FOR EXAMPLE, IS CAPABLE OF ACTING ON CONVICTION. A PERSON OF INTEGRITY CAN CONTROL IMPULSES AND APPETITES.
- BUT INTEGRITY ALSO COVERS SEVERAL OTHER MORAL TRAITS INDISPENSABLE TO NATIONAL SERVICE.

COURAGE

- A PERSON OF INTEGRITY POSSESSES MORAL COURAGE AND DOES WHAT IS RIGHT EVEN IF THE PERSONAL COST IS HIGH.

---

[49] "About the Air Force: Our Values" *United States Air Force - Airforce.com.* <http://www.airforce.com/learn-about/our-values/> (29 Apr. 2010). Used with permission.

HONESTY

- HONESTY IS THE HALLMARK OF THE MILITARY PROFESSIONAL BECAUSE IN THE MILITARY, OUR WORD MUST BE OUR BOND. WE DON'T PENCIL-WHIP TRAINING REPORTS, WE DON'T COVER UP TECH DATA VIOLATIONS, WE DON'T FALSIFY DOCUMENTS AND WE DON'T WRITE MISLEADING OPERATIONAL READINESS MESSAGES. THE BOTTOM LINE IS: WE DON'T LIE, AND WE CAN'T JUSTIFY ANY DEVIATION.

RESPONSIBILITY

- NO PERSON OF INTEGRITY IS IRRESPONSIBLE; A PERSON OF TRUE INTEGRITY ACKNOWLEDGES HIS/HER DUTIES AND ACTS ACCORDINGLY.

ACCOUNTABILITY

- NO PERSON OF INTEGRITY TRIES TO SHIFT THE BLAME TO OTHERS OR TAKE CREDIT FOR THE WORK OF OTHERS. "THE BUCK STOPS HERE" SAYS IT BEST.

JUSTICE

- A PERSON OF INTEGRITY PRACTICES JUSTICE. THOSE WHO DO SIMILAR THINGS MUST GET SIMILAR REWARDS OR SIMILAR PUNISHMENTS.

OPENNESS

- PROFESSIONALS OF INTEGRITY ENCOURAGE A FREE FLOW OF INFORMATION WITHIN THE ORGANIZATION. THEY SEEK FEEDBACK FROM ALL DIRECTIONS TO ENSURE THEY ARE FULFILLING KEY RESPONSIBILITIES, AND THEY ARE NEVER AFRAID TO ALLOW ANYONE AT ANY TIME TO EXAMINE HOW THEY DO BUSINESS.

SELF-RESPECT

- TO HAVE INTEGRITY IS ALSO TO RESPECT ONESELF AS A PROFESSIONAL AND A HUMAN BEING. A PERSON OF INTEGRITY DOES NOT BEHAVE IN WAYS THAT WOULD BRING DISCREDIT UPON HIMSELF/HERSELF OR THE ORGANIZATION TO WHICH HE/SHE BELONGS.

HUMILITY

- A PERSON OF INTEGRITY GRASPS AND IS SOBERED BY THE AWESOME TASK OF DEFENDING THE CONSTITUTION OF THE UNITED STATES OF AMERICA.

Summary

In the bridge metaphor, I have equated values with the massive concrete cable anchorages. Values are the immovable anchorage for leadership, serving as a keel to stabilize the organization as it is tossed in the storm, in the waves of change, uncertainty and turmoil. I offer two concluding thoughts.

First, these values drive ethical – or unethical – behaviors in the enterprise. Attention in detail to the implications of leadership and organizational behaviors – however small and inconsequential they may seem at the time – defines whether or not the values are real or imagined.

Do the stated values permeate the organization and drive its behaviors? I'm reminded of the words of Ben Franklin:

> *"For the want of a nail, the shoe was lost; for the want of a shoe the horse was lost; and for the want of a horse the rider*

was lost, being overtaken and slain by the enemy, all for the want of care about a horseshoe nail."[50]

Second, there are only two cable anchorages for the Mackinac Bridge. They have been in place now for nearly six decades. Businesses should take note:

> *"Core values in a visionary company form a rock-solid foundation and do not drift with the trends and fashions of the day; in some cases, the core values have remained intact for well over one hundred years."*[51]

The next chapter takes us into a consideration of the second key concept in our bridge model, Piers 19 and 20 and the twin towers attached to them, which I have described as: **Relationships[+].**

---

[50] "For the Want of a Nail ... by Benjamin Franklin." <http://www.quotedb.com/quotes/464> (June 2011).
[51] James C. Collins & Jerry I. Porras, *Built to Last: Successful Habits of Visionary Companies,* HarperCollins Publishers, Inc., New York, 2002, p. 8.

Chapter Five

Towers / Footings / Relationships[+]

"A friend at your back is like a bridge."

– Dutch Proverb

"Trust enables everything to move faster, more effortlessly, and with less conflict."

– Paul R. Lawrence & Robert Porter Lynch

"When people talk to us about the qualities they admire in leaders, they often use 'integrity' and 'character' as synonymous with honesty."

– James M. Kouzes & Barry Z. Posner

Relationships, integrity and awareness support leadership, just as the footings and towers support the suspension cables of the Mackinac Bridge.

In the bridge metaphor, the two load-bearing towers are relationships – personal relationships between corporate leaders, managers, employees, clients and customers. The main footings supporting those relationships are personal integrity and personal awareness, represented in this simple formula:

Relationships[+] = Personal Integrity + Personal Awareness

These very important facets of the model have been summarized as "Relationships⁺" in the diagram on page 94.

The key to the success of the Mackinac Bridge was the solid footings, the foundations on which the bridge superstructure was built, going all the way down to bedrock. Solid interpersonal relationships require solid personal integrity. Personal integrity cuts to the core of who we are. It's what we are when no one is looking. It embraces honesty and trustworthiness. Are we committed to truth? Are we trustworthy? Do we do what we say we will do? Can we be trusted to do what we say we will do? Do we consistently model and practice these behaviors? Or not?

Integrity

In a day and age when we are surrounded by numerous examples of moral failure, a fundamental meltdown in the personal integrity of business leaders and politicians, it is refreshing to reflect on the basics:

> "Integrity is a character trait. It is the willingness to do what is right even when no one is looking. It is the moral compass, the inner voice, the voice of self-control and the basis for the trust imperative in today's military. Integrity is the ability to hold together and properly regulate all of the elements of a personality. A person of integrity, for example, is capable of acting on conviction. A person of integrity can control impulses and appetites. But integrity also covers several other moral traits indispensable to national service (courage, honesty, responsibility, accountability, justice, openness, self-respect, humility)."[52]

The character trait of integrity also embraces honor. Chris Brady and Orrin Woodward in *Launching a Leadership Revolution: Mastering*

---

[52] Op. cit., "About the Air Force: Our Values."

the Five Levels of Influence point out that character and integrity, woven together, define honor. Jeff O'Leary, writing in *The Centurion Principles* defines honor as including "the virtues of integrity and honesty, self-denial, loyalty, and a servant's humility to those in authority above as well as a just and merciful heart to those below."[53]

Integrity is a personal attribute that embraces many other behavioral and moral qualities. In my consultancy, I do a lot of work with assessments. I have none that measure integrity. Perhaps that is because integrity must be lived. It is difficult to measure ... yet I know it when I see it.

Integrity is an asset that must be actively managed. It is not a constant. Integrity can be very quickly compromised if it is not given ongoing attention. *"... we found that those rated high in integrity were also rated high on assertiveness ... Those with high integrity were very effective at stepping forward and addressing difficult issues, confronting conflict, being direct, and facing up to difficult situations."*[54] Integrity takes a lifetime to build ... and it can be lost in a heartbeat.

I prefer to define personal integrity simply as the net sum of honesty and trustworthiness, shown in this simple illustration:

Personal Integrity = Honesty + Trustworthiness

Integrity: Honesty

Trust and honesty are the two identical twins which define personal integrity. Let's first consider honesty:

---

[53] Chris Brady,and Orrin Woodward, *Launching a Leadership Revolution: Mastering the Five Levels of Influence* (New York, NY: Business Plus, 2005) p. 48.

[54] John H. Zenger & Joseph R. Folkman, *The Extraordinary Leader: Turning Good Managers into Great Leaders* (New York: McGraw Hill, 2009) p. 178.

"In almost every survey we've conducted, honesty has been selected more often than any other leadership characteristic; overall, it emerges as the single most important ingredient in the leader-constituency relationship ... Since the first time we conducted our studies in the early 1980s, honesty has been at the top of the list ... That nearly 90 percent of constituents want their leaders to be honest above all else is a message that all leaders must take to heart."[55]

Simply, honesty is telling the truth. In a day and age when truth is becoming increasingly difficult to find, it is absolutely refreshing when we find it. As a character trait, honesty must be a consistent behavior. The measure of honesty? Never tell a lie.

Integrity: Trust

Integrity is the other twin which – working with honesty – defines personal integrity:

"Trust's great value can be achieved only in an organization where basic values are reinforced with concrete, measurable behavioral actions. Only then can organizations reach new heights in relationships."[56]

This reality is captured in this graphic:

Values → Behaviors → Trust → Strong Relationships

---

[55] James M. Kouzes and Barry Z. Posner, The Leadership Challenge, 3rd edition (New York, NY: John Wiley & Sons, Inc., 2002) p. 27.
[56] Paul R. Lawrence and Robert Porter Lynch, "Leadership and the Structure of Trust,". *The European Business Review*, May-June 2011, p. 18.

Trustworthiness is a fundamental aspect of integrity and is an important part of the footings that support solid relationships. Webster defines trustworthy as "worthy of confidence, dependable, reliable." Galford and Drapeau plumbed the depths of the concept of trustworthiness in their definition of trust:[57]

$$\text{Trust} = \frac{\text{Credibility} + \text{Reliability} + \text{Intimacy}}{\text{Self-interest}}$$

Please note that in this formula, trust is inversely proportional to self-interest: trust is easily diminished where self-interest is high. In the world of business, I see far too many business leaders who are narcissists. Their self-interest defines them. It consumes them. It erodes trust.

Narcissism – Guaranteed Erosion of Trust

One of the insights I've gained from four decades in business is that if there were a Center for Disease Control for the executive suites in America, probably the number one pandemic would be narcissism.

> "With their need for power, status, prestige, and glamour, many narcissistic personalities eventually end up in leadership positions. The ability of narcissists to manipulate others and their capacity to establish rapid, if shallow, relationships serve them well as they move up the organizational ladder ... Unfortunately, power, prestige, and status are typically more important to these people than a serious commitment to organizational goals and performance. Because narcissists are motivated by selfishness, their successes are ephemeral."[58]

---

[57] Robert Galford and Anne Seibold Drapeau, *The Trusted Leader* (New York: Free Press, 2002).

[58] Manfred Kets de Vries, *The Leader on the Couch* (West Sussex, England: John Wiley & Sons, Ltd., 2006) p. 28.

This kind of personality flaw lies at the heart of many business failures (see Chapter Five of the author's previous book *Business Model Innovation*).[59]

Two Sad Stories

Many years ago, before I had children of my own, I was at a lake with a friend who was enjoying his young nephew very much. The boy was four years old and took great delight in energetically throwing himself, launching his body through the air from a picnic table, confident that his uncle would catch him. It was an amazing visual illustration of total trust.

Sadly, as I watched that trust lived out, I was reminded of a story I had read shortly before that day. A father urged his young son to jump into his arms. When he jumped, his father let him fall, and said, "Let that be a lesson to you to never trust anyone."

Even more sadly, recently I ran into a businessman whom I knew when he was a young boy growing up two doors down the street. As we visited over lunch, I sketched for him the business model Building Bridges to the Future®. With a tone of disappointment in his voice, he told me that in over two decades as a businessman he had never had a boss he could trust.

In the context of these two sad stories about the lack of trust in the home and in the workplace, consider this wisdom:

> "What too few executives seem to understand is that in a faster moving, more rapidly changing world, we need more trust, certainly not more distrust, to keep a sense of order and balance. Trust is the one thing that's essential in a stormy sea.

---

[59] John & Imelda Butler and Melvin D. Nelson, *Business Model Innovation: Proven Strategies That Actually Work* (Sevierville, TN: Insight Publishing, 2010). Available on Amazon.

Yet just the opposite has happened, trust has gone into precipitous decline at the very time we need more of it. "[60]

Personal Awareness of Self & Others

The discussion of integrity, honesty and trustworthiness sets the stage for a discussion of awareness – another foundational quality of strong relationships. Personal awareness includes keen self-awareness and other-awareness, key components of emotional intelligence:

Personal Awareness = Self-awareness + Other-awareness

One of my avocations is military history. As a pilot, I am especially intrigued with the harrowing experiences of fighter pilots in combat. One of the skills they must acquire to survive in a combat setting is a refined sense of situational awareness – closely paying attention to what is going on around them while skillfully flying their aircraft. A closely related skill is to be able to think through the dynamics of the fight in three dimensions, while adroitly managing the kinetic energy of speed and the potential energy of altitude. It is a complex, instantaneously choreographed ballet with their life on the line.

When I apply these principles to the choreography of personal and professional relationships, I think in terms of a personal relationship model with three dimensions: self-awareness and other-awareness, which together inform my chosen behaviors, my personal conduct in the situation.

---

[60] Paul R. Lawrence and Robert Porter Lynch, "Leadership and the Structure of Trust," *The European Business Review* (May-June 2011): 17.

3D Personal Relationship Model

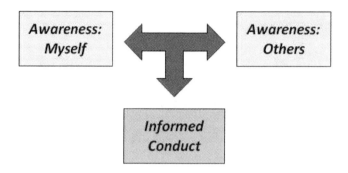

Two dimensions of awareness / one dimension of action

© Copyright 2010 Executive Management Systems, Inc.

Effective situational awareness in personal and professional relationships means that I am continually aware of myself, others, and the range of choices I have in responding to stimuli.

This informed, deliberate response is what Stephen Covey had in mind when he defined proactivity as the moment between stimulus and response, the time for us to exercise initiative and take responsibility for our actions. In this moment, juxtaposed between stimulus and response, we have the freedom to choose.[61]

When our conduct is the result of a deliberate choice informed by in-depth awareness of our self and of others, we can be very effective in building relationships which support effective personal leadership.

---

[61] Stephen R. Covey, *The 7 Habits of Highly Effective People* (New York: Simon & Schuster, 1989) pp. 71-72.

This 3D Personal Leadership Model embraces the four emotional intelligence leadership competencies[62] of self-awareness, self-management, social awareness and relationship management.

My Very Good Friend John

I want to include in this chapter a personal example of how these factors defined a personal and professional relationship that was both very strong and very deep.

I first met John Butler in 2006, at a professional consulting conference in Phoenix, hosted by an organization I had joined the previous summer. The context of our discussion was a professional development program John had developed called "Odyssey: The Business of Consulting." It was a real draw for me. I had taken my practice to a point where I had been searching for a strategy to take me to the next level. As a member of five professional networks, I had a vision of where I wanted to go and I had been searching for a solid strategy. Until I talked with John, I had no clearly defined strategy on how to move my business to the next level.

When the five-day session was offered in January 2007, I was there, and worked through the experience with John and Imelda Butler, Rolando Marchis, and four other consultants enrolled in that Odyssey class. I got to know John, Imelda, and Rolando as friends.

My friend John was a man of faith. He was a committed husband and proud father, a good family man. He was a man of action. High energy. Intelligent. Thoughtful. Creative. Fun. Visionary. Action-oriented. Kind. Direct. Positive. Realistic. Entertaining. Committed. Values-driven.

---

[62]Daniel Goleman, Richard Boyatzis, and Annie McKee, *"Primal Leadership: Learning to Lead with Emotional Intelligence"* (Boston: Harvard Business School Press, 2002) pp. 253-256.

Chuck Swindoll, in his character sketch and study of King David (*David: A Man of Passion & Destiny*), identifies four levels of friendship, which I've captured in the illustration below: acquaintances, casual friends, close friends, and intimate friends. Swindoll defines intimate friends as "those few people with whom we have regular contact and a deep commitment. We are not only open and vulnerable with these people, we anxiously await their counsel. Intimate friends are just as free to criticize and to correct us as they are to embrace and encourage, because trust and mutual understanding has been established between them."[63]

The kind of friendship that King David and his friend Jonathan enjoyed was a level four friendship ... and that's the kind of friendship I came to enjoy with John Butler.

Four Levels of Friendship

One of the things that took our friendship to level four was a collaborative project we took on in the spring of 2010 – an executive briefing scheduled in September 2010 entitled *"Is Your Business Model Right for These Times?"* As a key part of this executive briefing, we would offer copies of a book we would co-author on business models.

Early in our first in-depth conversation in 2006 – John, Imelda and Mel – the topic turned to a discussion of models: simplified

---

[63] Charles R. Swindoll, *David: A Man of Passion and Destiny* (Dallas, Texas: Word Publishing, Inc., 1997) p. 251.

frameworks to help us understand and manage complex issues. When I described the Building Bridges to the Future® model so thoroughly described in this book, John was impressed. He saw this business model – in his words – as a "model on models." We had many conversations about it. It was a driving force in his suggestion that we co-author a book.

John was passionate about models – their value, their elegant yet profound transforming simplicity. He continually spoke to this, and the need for them in the world of business. In this book, we married our thinking about models, collaborating on a work that took our thinking to a new level.[64]

We set the goal on May 12 and committed to completing the book by August 1. We worked very closely to make it happen and were in frequent contact by phone and email. At times, my Skype mic would go to mute, and John would raise his voice, "Mel, I lost you. Mel are you there? MEL? MEL??" ... at which point Imelda would come running in from the next office to see what John wanted. We laughed about that many times, suggesting to John that he should communicate more clearly: Imelda was "Mel 1" and I was "Mel 2".

By July 23, a Friday, we had the book about 85% completed, with a lot of final editing, tweaking, indexing, and final packaging to be done. That day, we had a Skype conference call with the publisher to brainstorm and finalize the title of the book. We chose *Business Model Innovation: Proven Strategies That Actually Work.*

On that three-way Skype conference call, we had a very productive discussion, but we kept getting cut off from the publisher. When that happened, John and I would wait until we could reconnect, but it gave the two of us a chance to talk 1:1 about the direction of our three-way conversation. I was concerned that

---

[64] Op. cit., Butler and Nelson.

we cover the ground we had to cover in the time we had with the publisher. At one point, John gently nudged me in a 1:1 interlude by saying, "Let's stay in the present moment, and see how this conversation develops – I really like where he is going." This was so like John, deftly making a point to achieve better results in a "master practitioner" communications moment.

The concept of PMA – "present moment awareness" – which John often highlighted is exactly as it suggests: staying very alert to all that is going on right now, absorbing and processing it while resisting the urge to race ahead to what's next. This principle is one that is so important in building highly connective relationships with business owners and executives as clients ... and it was so like John to be continually reinforcing the Odyssey Master Class principles which he felt were so important.

To achieve our aggressive goal of completing the book in a ten-week timeframe, John and Imelda were often up in the early morning, 4 or 5 A.M., to get their part done. They were up very early on that Saturday, July 24 to review the latest edits I'd sent them. They both felt very good about where the book was heading with the latest copy and edits.

John and I had an appointment to talk early Monday, July 26 to put the book on track for completion that week, before "the holidays" during the first two weeks of August. Before I left for work that Monday morning, I was reading in the book I mentioned earlier (Charles Swindoll – *David: A Man of Passion & Destiny*). The principle that stuck with me that day was that one of God's gifts to us is that He does not let us know what is in the future. This was an interesting reminder to enjoy our present moment, tying in with the conversation I'd had with John on Friday.

I called John at our appointed time that Monday morning. No answer. Stranger yet, no email from John that day ... it was totally unlike him. I took the call from Rolando that afternoon to let me know that John had passed away on Sunday. I was shocked. I've lost friends and family to death before ... but I've never felt the blow of death to that extent.

The blow was great for several reasons. It was totally unexpected. Our collaboration had been so intense to achieve the goal of completing our book by August 1. Our friendship was very close, our camaraderie was unique, our shared values and personal bond were deep.

Truly, not knowing the future is one of God's remarkable gifts to us. Had I known the future when I was talking with John on July 23, it would have been a miserable moment for me. I could not have enjoyed the time we had that day.

As I think back to that last conversation I had with John, and his encouragement for me to stay in the present moment, I am reminded of the lyrics of the song "We Have This Moment, Today." The key thought of that song is that we have the opportunity to hold tight to the here and now, and savor the moment. Yesterday is in the past, and the future? Well, who knows? Enjoy life in the present.

I have a lot of rich memories of time spent with my very good friend John, time that then was "today" ... the present moment. And that is a life lesson I'll never forget: live life with a healthy focus on the here and now ... in the present.

I'm reminded of the words of Winston Churchill, "It is a mistake to look too far ahead. Only one link of the chain of destiny can be handled at a time."

Summary

Our personal capabilities as professionals are heavily dependent on our ability to build personal relationships on the foundation of our personal integrity, combined with high awareness of self and others. Our personal integrity is heavily dependent on our honesty and trustworthiness.

Integrity is the basis for strong interpersonal relationships. Combined with emotional intelligence, it is a bedrock platform for personal relationships.

The three simple formulas set forth in this chapter capture and underscore these very important fundamental truths. These thoughts are summarized in the table below:

Towers	Footings	
Relationships⁺ =	**Personal Integrity**	Honesty
		Trustworthiness
	Personal Awareness	Self-awareness
		Other-awareness

These first two systems (covered in Chapters Four and Five) – **Values⁺** and **Relationships⁺** – establish the structure to support the next element of the bridge model – **Leadership⁺** – to be covered in the next chapter.

Leaders who are not anchored in strong values and supported by relationships based on personal integrity and emotional intelligence ... ultimately fail. A leader must not violate the laws of gravity regardless of his or her position or authority. Leaders must not violate the laws of physics regardless of how much they are in charge.

Chapter Six

Suspension Cables / Leadership⁺

"Character is the center pole of the leadership tent."
— John H. Zenger & Joseph R. Folkman

"Example is not the main thing in influencing others, it is the only thing."
— Albert Schweitzer

In the *Building Bridges to the Future*® metaphor, the suspension cables are leadership performance and executive performance. With a suspension bridge, the total weight of the bridge spans and all the traffic hangs on the suspension cables. In building a bridge to the future for any enterprise, the total weight of the strategy, action and results hangs on leadership.

Suspension Cables and Lessons in Leadership

The spans and traffic of the Mackinac Bridge are supported by two 24½-inch suspension cables. These suspension cables were "spun" with 41,000 miles of steel wire. This effort bound roughly 340 wires into one strand, extending from one cable anchorage, up over the two main towers, to the other cable anchorage. Each cable has 37 strands, with a total of 12,350 wires.[65]

---

[65] Op. cit., Modern Marvels.

Leadership lesson #1: In the bridge metaphor, the 41,000 miles of steel wire at the core of the suspension cables represent character.

To ensure the integrity of the suspension cables, they were enclosed in a protective sheath, after first being coated with a red lead, anti-corrosive paste. The primary threat to suspension cable integrity is rust and corrosion. There is an on-going, continual effort to monitor the integrity of these cables over the life of the bridge and to protect against corrosion.

Leadership lesson #2: In the bridge metaphor, the protective sheath and the red lead anti-corrosive paste represent conscience.

A well-grounded conscience protects against character erosion, just as the anti-corrosive paste and sheath protect the all-important load-bearing cables. Recent inspections show that the integrity of the suspension cables remains very high after fifty years in service.[66]

Switching from the physical bridge to the business metaphor, a logical question is, "What is being done in your enterprise to ensure the integrity of leadership over the long haul?" Think about it:

Character + Conscience = Leadership Integrity.

Leadership lesson #3: Leadership development is not an individual sport, reserved for the top echelon of leaders in an enterprise. It is a team sport.

Reflect on this for a minute. Constructing two suspension cables to support the 8,600 foot center bridge span required 41,000 miles of steel wire spun into two 24½-inch suspension cables with 300

---

[66] Mike Fornes, *Images of America: Mackinac Bridge* (Chicago: Arcadia Publishing, 2007) p. 79.

men working 12-hour back-to-back shifts over 2½ months.[67] This leadership backbone / suspension cable was not the result of the sole efforts of one or two people. There was a team of 300 totally committed to the task. It was not a result that was achieved overnight. It was a result of high energy and total engagement, focused over a long period of time that achieved the goal.

So it is with leadership. Leadership skills are not developed overnight. Leadership development is not a one-time event. It requires an on-going commitment.

Leadership Development

Leadership development is critical to an effective strategy, and must begin prior to the development of strategy. The second span of the bridge model – team engagement (see p. 109) – usually includes the first five half-day sessions of the full-blown leadership development program. Strategy development follows this important step of initial leadership development.

Recently, my wife and I took a cruise to Alaska that included a trip through the interior. One of the highlights of the trip was our introduction to Iditarod Racing and the process of training sled dogs. The racer whom we met had 150 dogs in various stages of development to produce a team of nine. It was inspiring to see the team's excitement and energy. In one demonstration, they pull the trainer at high speed around a one-mile track on a four-wheeler with its motor removed. The stock brakes had been replaced with oversized brakes, necessary for stopping the high-energy dog team. While waiting to go, the four-wheeler had to be roped to a stake to hold it. The acceleration to ~25 mph was amazingly swift. The key was the lead dog, which put his head down and aggressively pulled. This action triggered the in-bred response in the others on the team

---

[67] Op. cit., Modern Marvels.

to pull. A good racing team is spurred on by the conduct of the lead dog ... and relies on the lead dog, which leads by example.

One of my client CEOs was firmly convinced that *"Leadership development is for the many ... not for the few."* As we rolled out their leadership development program, there were dozens of key individuals in the program. The best results in corporate leadership development are a direct outcome of this approach: The Iditarod sled dog breeder/trainer/ racer had 150+ dogs in his racing talent pool to produce a team of nine, with one selected as the leader at the top.

Too many times, the paradigm which prevails in executive suites is *"Leadership development for the few, not the many"* and strategic opportunities to broadly develop organizational talent are lost. Warren Bennis and Burt Nanus touched on this when they pointed out that one of five "recurring myths that ... discourage potential leaders from 'taking charge' ... [is that] leadership exists only at the top of an organization."[68] The reality is that leadership in an effective organization permeates the entire organization.

Executive Development

An integral part of leadership development is executive coaching. Executives looking to enhance their leadership effectiveness – and the success of their organization – benefit from Executive Management Systems' dynamic, powerful coaching framework. It's all about chemistry ... the chemistry of integrity, relationships, and leadership: an integrated system of footings, towers, suspension cables.

Built on the proven premise that solid relationships within an organization are imperative, especially in today's high-tech, fast-

---

[68] Warren Bennis & Burt Nanus, *Leaders: The Strategies for Taking Charge* (New York: Harper & Row, Publishers, Inc., 1985) pp. 221, 224.

paced business environment, Executive Management Systems' executive development program follows two key steps:

- Improve self-awareness
- Deepen other-awareness

Through research-based assessments and seasoned leadership insights, EMS helps executives best develop and implement their personal plan for enhanced leadership and organizational success.

Developing Emerging Talent

The effective development of leadership talent in an organization includes two synergistic and catalytic spheres:

- The development and practice of leadership skills in a team setting; and
- The development of individual leadership talent in a personal coaching setting.

These two spheres work together to achieve results unattainable if either is pursued singularly. The catalytic chemistry for comprehensive talent development will not occur unless both spheres are integrated side by side to create the "learning moments" that lead to lasting, profound transformational learning.

A critical need in business leadership is emotional intelligence (EQ). Some aspects of emotional intelligence are best conveyed in a team development session, and then reinforced in personal coaching sessions. For example, in the table below, the two EQ competencies of social expertness and personal influence are best developed when concurrently addressed in both arenas. The most effective return on a leadership team's investment of time and energy for talent development is to intertwine the team classroom sessions with individual 1:1 coaching.

The reasons for this are many. The team leadership development session introduces concepts which can be learned and practiced in a safe environment with peers, in role-play sessions to reinforce each set of leadership skills. The real polish on these skills comes in the personal coaching, which allows the coached professional to drive these skills into the bedrock of their personal leadership vision and conduct. Most importantly, both team and individual learning environments are required to develop five EQ competencies[69]:

1. Self-awareness & control
2. Empathy
3. Social expertness
4. Personal influence
5. Mastery of vision

The team leadership development introduces a variety of assessments which give participants a chance to start building out a comprehensive picture of who they are – leadership style, communication styles, innovation style (to name a few) – and how the team can explore and capitalize on each of these dimensions. The resulting aggregate understanding of self and others – relation to each other in a team setting – is a very valuable outcome of the integrated team leadership sessions and private coaching sessions.

Personal Coaching

The private coaching sessions utilize the assessment platforms already covered in the first five team leadership development sessions. Additional assessment platforms are introduced which are more comprehensive, more intrusive and more valuable. The focus

---

[69] Adele B. Lynn, *The Emotional Intelligence Activity Book* (American Management Association: New York, 2002) pp. 3-4.

of these coaching sessions is to bring out the talent within – both already-known and newly-discovered talents. The focus is not to put in what is not there.

The three goals of this personal leadership coaching are:

1. To develop an individual's leadership talent
2. To increase confidence, breadth of thought & action, personal & organizational effectiveness
3. To personally model effective leadership skills

Key strategies to achieve these goals include:

- A self-directed learning experience
- Within a bounded environment
- Enabled by a proven set of tools

3D Leadership Model

The 3D Leadership Model embraces two dimensions of understanding and one dimension of action, as shown in the diagram below. You will note that this diagram – with the exception of the title – is the same diagram presented in the last chapter (3D Relationship Model). Leadership and relationships go hand-in-hand and have three dimensions.

Dimension #1 is self-awareness. It is insight into your behaviors, talents, and your uniqueness. Dimension #2 is other-awareness. It is insights into others, their behaviors, talents, and how they are uniquely different from you, as well as things they may have in common with you.

Dimension #3 is the intelligent conduct you choose which is informed by your understanding of yourself, others and best leadership practices. Those best leadership practices are defined and initially acquired in the team leadership development sessions. The best leadership practices are polished in the focused 1:1 coaching sessions.

This integrated, 3D Leadership Model zeros in on the four emotional intelligence leadership skills defined by Goleman: Self-awareness, self-management, social awareness and relationship management.[70]

3D Personal Leadership Model

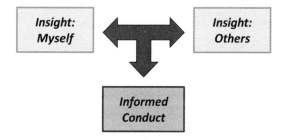

Two dimensions of understanding / one dimension of action

© Executive Management Systems, Inc. 2010

---

[70] Op. cit., Goleman, Boyatzis, and McKee, pp. 253-256.

Personal Leadership Vision

Twenty-five years ago, I developed a statement of leadership principles, which characterized my approach to business and life leadership. Developing this personal leadership vision was an important first step to my development of the *"Building Bridges to the Future*®*"* model. This critical first step served as a catalyst and preceded the development of the integrated model by nearly two decades.

This personal statement of my leadership philosophy has served me well as a touchstone for my decision-making and personal focus in direction-setting. Because the development of a personal leadership vision has been so helpful to me in my career, I make development of one an integral exercise and a key deliverable in my executive coaching with clients.

This written, personal leadership vision and plan is a living document, which will follow coaching recipients through their career. The point is to get started ... and to keep updating it. Each of these personal vision statements is unique in format and content. It is custom-tailored to and by the individual.

It is a very personal document. I caution participants to share it sparingly and very carefully – perhaps with their spouse, with other mentors, and, if a high trust level exists, with their employer. Rather than sharing the specific content of their plan with a broad audience, I challenge participants to verbally and behaviorally infuse their vision into all that they do ... to live their vision and adjust it as they continue to learn.

The coaching framework is typically completed over a 16-week period. This schedule sustains the necessary momentum for development while allowing time for reading, reflection, and reinforcement of the leadership curriculum through on-line review.

This contemplative, reflective process is fundamental to developing the written personal leadership vision and plan.

Personal Vision – One Business Owner's Story

Two years ago, I was retained by a business owner to help him take his business to the next level. After a thoughtful diagnostic session with this president and his number two, I suggested seven steps we could take together to improve his business operations. He chose to engage me for team leadership development the first year. That year was the most profitable year he had had in thirty-one years of business operations.

The following year he chose to focus on executive coaching for his personal leadership development. One of the first things I asked him to do before we began was to read the semi-final draft of this book (*Building Bridges*). After reading the book he said: "This will be more than business coaching – it is an exercise in life coaching. I like the breadth – it includes both business and personal aspects."

He went on to comment about the book, "It is about life strategy ... One of the ways this life strategy played out was in business. To sum up the book, in a nutshell, it is about a life well-ordered, intentionality in all things. It is interesting to see intentional living implemented from the get-go – it plays out with huge dividends. It is very thought-provoking ... I should start sometime. Age 51 isn't too late."

This individual is a successful businessman. He is a proven team player and a collaborative leader with his employees. One of the factors we discussed in the coaching was a low sense of self. He was self-critical and had a hard time recognizing and discussing his numerous talents and strengths. After working through the coaching exercise, he had this to say (Note the shift in his thinking over a ten-week period):

This has been a very encouraging exercise. It has helped me recognize personal strengths that I did not recognize previously. Until now, it has been difficult for me to say a whole lot positive about myself.

The positive attributes I am now seeing in myself boost my confidence. A lot of what I did previously was fear-based. What if I don't have all of these things done right? What if ____? What if ____? What if _____? I now have more confidence that we can figure it out and that things will be in place.

The "hard-worker" parts of my vision and skill set reflect my father. I always say I don't have to prove anything to anyone ... except to myself and my Dad ... but I have less to prove now. With more self-confidence, I will not be driven the same.

It will be easier to give out praise. I sense that I am going to be happier ... and those around me will also be happier (my co-workers, family and others). When I address issues that need to be fixed in my business, I will fix things in my personal life. The reverse is also true.

I have often asked myself, "Why do I love learning so much?" I now know that a love of knowledge and learning is my #1 motivator. What does that suggest I should be doing in the future? More and more, I am seeing that I am where I should be and I am doing what I should be doing.

I am going to keep my personal leadership vision front and center. It is a useful, working document, practical in everyday life. It will be very effective ... and I will keep it fresh. It is not just words. It is very real – all of these things are really me – and I know they are real.

Values, Behaviors, Culture and Leadership Development

In the context of leadership development in this chapter, I want to go back to the discussion in the previous two chapters to build a systemic view of values, behaviors, culture and leadership development.

This is a very significant point: Left unaddressed, a sick culture trumps brilliant strategy every time. A sick culture is the elephant in the room, which must be addressed for strategic initiatives to succeed. Well done, leadership development becomes a change agent to engage a sick culture and restore health.

Values drive behaviors. Behaviors define culture. Leadership development and executive coaching – working together – can equip business leaders with a new skill set and a new mindset. These in turn define a "new normal" for leadership in the enterprise … and this can influence a shift in the organizational culture (to be discussed further in the next chapter).

This concept and principle is captured in the following diagram, which could be entitled *"Setting the Tone at the Top"*:

Values → Behaviors → Culture

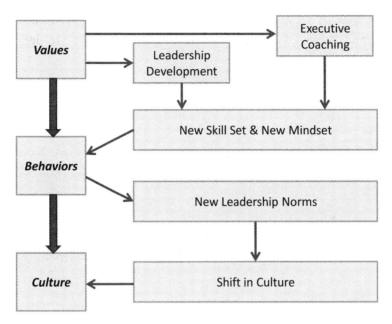

© Executive Management Systems, Inc. 2011

Summary

Let's revisit, for just a moment, the overall bridge/business analogy. We have covered the first three systems in suspension bridge construction: the cable anchorages, the towers and footings, and the suspension cables. These correlate to the elements in our bridge model: **Values[+]**, **Relationships[+]** and **Leadership[+]**.

In building a bridge to the future, the total weight of the strategy, action and results hangs on values-driven leadership, which is supported by strong relationships grounded in personal integrity and high levels of emotional intelligence.

With each of the bridge systems and business model elements we have discussed to this point, we now are ready to discuss the bridge deck, the spans of **Strategy[+]**.

Chapter Seven

Spans of Strategy⁺

"To see what everyone else has seen and think what no one else has thought ..."

– Nobel laureate Albert Szent-Györgyi

"A bridge represents this triumph of man, represents the fulfillment of a concept or vision, the expression of one man's dream."

– David B. Steinman and Sara Ruth Watson

Bridges are a time machine. They enable mind-travel to the future. In my work, I've defined five very useful spans for building a bridge to the future. These five spans represent key, sequential steps in developing the bridge to the future:

1. Strategic Thinking
2. Team Engagement
3. Strategy Development
4. Change Leadership
5. Execution

The spans of the bridge are the road deck that conveys people across the bridge, from where they are to where they want to go. In the bridge metaphor, these five spans of strategy – coupled with the bridge structure – can propel an organization from where it is to where it wants to go.

Strategic Thinking & the Mackinac Bridge

Strategic thinking starts in the mind of one. It is personal vision that drives corporate vision. It is personal insight that drives corporate insight. What starts as a spark of insight in the mind of one can be fanned into a flame of passion to engage the many.

The comment of Nobel laureate Albert Szent-Györgyi, *"To see what everyone else has seen and think what no one else has thought"* is a good definition of the critical role of innovation in strategic thinking.

Innovation requires breaking out of the rut of paradigm-constrained thinking. Laurence J. Peter said it well: *"A rut is a grave with the ends knocked out ..."* Many confuse the edge of their rut – their mind-limiting paradigms – with their horizon of possibilities. They do not look beyond the edge of that "mind rut" and thus constrain the scope of their vision.

The notion of crossing the straits of Mackinac was a dream that many had, but none of them had the personal drive, leadership and know-how to execute it ... until David Steinman showed up.

The completion of the Brooklyn Bridge in 1883 spurred one store owner in St. Ignace, Michigan to feature an illustration of the Brooklyn Bridge in his advertising and labeled it, *"Proposed bridge across the Straits of Mackinac."* The history of the bridge identifies a variety of events and much discussion by many over two generations – in 1884, 1888, 1920, 1923, 1934, 1937, and 1947 – but with no tangible results, no definitive action.

The Mackinac Bridge was completed in 1957 – and as with all great projects and vision – it started as the idea of one. The son of immigrants of obscure background, Dr. David B. Steinman grew up in New York City in the shadow of the Brooklyn Bridge. That suspension bridge made a lasting impression on him. Over four decades, Steinman developed a reputation as an outstanding designer of suspension bridges. His career and life-focus were set in motion by the images in his mind and the dreams of his youth. He first took a look at the Mackinac Straits in the thirties in his quest for challenging bridge projects.

By 1950, he had firmly established his reputation as a suspension bridge expert, having completed 400-plus projects. So clear and compelling was his personal vision to span the Straits of Mackinac with a suspension bridge of his design that he committed $250,000 of his own funds to complete the early design of the bridge. He was a man of vision and action.

Strategic Thinking – The First Span of Strategy

Since strategic thinking starts in the mind of the leader, my job is to draw out that picture inside his/her head. What is that picture? Drawing out that picture, painting it in color with clarity and crisp detail is the important first step in building a bridge to the future.

The prime mover for drawing out a business leader's strategic thinking is conversation coupled with a listening ear. John Drakeford captured this concept well when he wrote of a speaker's comment, *"How can I know what I think until I hear myself say it?'* He was obviously saying he needed someone to listen to him to be able to come to a better self-understanding ... Men need to test their thoughts. The inner world of ideas must be exteriorized and examined to discover if they will stand up in the world of reality. One of the best ways of doing this is by the 'test of verbalization.' The simple process of expressing ideas helps to clarify them."[71]

---

[71] Op. cit., Drakeford, p. 119.

This is the heart of the process to define the strategic thinking of a leader:

1. Conversation driven by the business leader,
2. Spurred by provocative questions from the executive consultant's active mind,
3. Coupled with the consultant's listening ear that
4. Captures the concepts in the words of the speaker.

These words and concepts are then massaged and refined until they come into a crystal clear and simplified focus ... and that is the essence of the first span of strategy: strategic thinking.

In my experience, this discussion will many times find the business leader verbalizing the content of his/her strategic thoughts for the first time. It is a rewarding place to be.

Bringing these thoughts out and into a sharp focus is the critical first step in strategy development.

Leadership Team Engagement – The Second Span of Strategy

The vision of building a bridge to the future starts in the mind of the leader. Achieving it requires the engagement of many. The Mackinac Bridge that started in the mind of one took an army of 2,500 to build.

The second span of strategy – team engagement – initially engages a leadership team which may vary in size from five executives to fifteen executives and key managers. The team engagement begins with an introduction to the CEO's newly-clarified strategic thinking. This seed for strategy development will again be revisited in the third span of strategy. But before the leadership team is ready to tackle the development of strategy, the right leadership environment must be created.

Creating this environment includes a focus on revitalizing interpersonal relationships on the leadership team, improved self- and other-awareness, and firming up personal leadership principles. Typically involving five half-day sessions, the team engagement provides the opportunity to get a sense of the organizational culture at the top and begin to align the team to focus on innovation and the attendant required leadership culture.

Since this part of the process is so critical to success in the next span – strategy development – it cannot be ignored.

Leadership Team Resources

In my experience, teams bring only three resources to the table – time, energy and talent. Good resource management sets the stage for success – good time management, good energy management, and good talent management.

Team Resource / Asset Management

Time + Energy + Talent = Team Assets

- Good time management →
- Good energy management →
- Good talent management

Good time management is a resource management strategy that is well-served by good team energy management and good team talent management.

Effective strategy development is backed by a commitment of resources. The Tacoma Narrows Bridge was a bridge that failed in the forties. The consensus of experts is that it was too light, too thin and too long. Many times efforts to define visionary business strategy fail because the effort is short on commitment of the necessary leadership resources – time, talent, and / or energy.

Team Engagement – Energy Management & Mental Ju-Jitsu

I've spent 30 years of my professional career in the energy business. Early in my career, I was given the Nikola Tesla Award by Westinghouse Electric for my work in energy management. Energy management was a theme and strategy that moved me forward throughout my career. I sought to leverage and maximize the positive energy in individuals, teams and organizations – while at the same time dissipating and diverting negative energy, or – better yet – converting the momentum of negative energy to positive energy.

One of my mentors used to talk about using mental ju-jitsu. That advice has stuck with me for a good many years. When I think of it, I think back to my days in high school when I had a strong interest in self-defense strategies. Although I had not taken a course in ju-jitsu, I had read about the basic principles and "knew" a couple of dramatic moves. One night after swimming team practice, I shared my newfound knowledge with my team mates. As we were talking about a move to flip an attacker on his back, I had a chance to demonstrate my insight. I asked one of my team mates to simulate an aggressive situation and start pushing me in the chest. In translating my head knowledge into reality, I backed up a step or two until the timing was right. When the "attacker" was just about to shift his weight to his right foot, I swiftly kicked the outside of that leg with my left foot, moving his right leg far to his left, taking him off balance while I pulled on his lapel to put him on the ground, flat on his back, faster than I can tell you about it. I do not know who was more surprised – him, me, or my teammates who were watching.

The principle of this self-defense move is to capture the aggressive, negative energy directed at you, and use it to redefine and reshape the situation. Mental ju-jitsu helps us redefine negative energy as opportunity – opportunity to see another point of view, opportunity to solve a problem, opportunity to collaborate.

Energy management is a critical discipline for executive teams as they develop business strategy. There are two kinds of energy – positive and negative. In developing strategy, positive energy must be found, nurtured, developed, and maximized. Negative energy must be dissipated or – better yet – morphed into positive energy.

Once the positive energy is identified, it must be aligned. Two equal forces pulling in the same direction yield twice the power. Two equal forces aligned in opposite directions create stalemate. Have you ever noticed that – generally speaking – when we hitch up a team of horses, usually we have them pointed in the same direction? Unless we achieve the same result in human endeavors, we're not practicing good energy management.

Team Engagement – Talent Management

Talent management goes hand-in-hand with energy management as an effective means to engage executive teams in developing vision-driven strategy. This vital part of team engagement involves assessing the leadership culture and the communications culture of the team. Additionally, it involves strengthening the leadership and communication skills in preparation for strategy development.

What is the executive team's leadership and communications culture? What are the undeveloped talents of the executive team's leadership and communications portfolio? How does the team innovate? How can we better leverage the diversity of team members' skills? What must be done to "clear the air" and immediately enable the executive team to function more effectively?

Executive Management Systems is adept at talent assessment and guiding businesses in tuning up existing teams — to achieve a healthier team culture and improved long-term performance. In developing business strategy, this team engagement, alignment, and team resource management has to start at the top. I've had clients tell me that this stage has been "a healing process" and it is the critical step that they had to complete before they were able to tackle strategy development. It is truly a defining moment when – as a result of the perspectives and insight generated in this stage – a team member will offer a heart-felt, life-changing apology for holding a flawed mental image of the team. I've been there when those moments occur ... and it literally sends shivers down my spine.

Business success is a logical outcome of effective teamwork. Effective teamwork is a result of leveraging diversity in team members' styles and talent in innovation, leadership, listening and communication. Leveraging this diversity to strengthen team performance requires awareness in two dimensions – awareness of self and awareness of others. This linkage is clearly seen in the Building Bridges to the Future® diagram, with the awareness factors shown in the footings, and the leadership skills in the suspension strategy, together supporting the five spans for the bridge.

Strategy Development – The Third Span of Strategy

Only when the first two steps are completed can the team begin to build the third span of the bridge: the development of strategy. This is where the heavy lifting occurs in strategy development. This phase typically includes at least six sessions with the leadership team.

It is in this phase where the leadership team is engaged in the expansion, further development of the CEO's initial vision. It is critical that the initial vision now becomes a shared vision, as the leadership team becomes engaged in the verbalization and creation of how the vision is to be focused, clarified, defined and achieved.

"There is no more powerful engine driving an organization toward excellence and long-range success than an attractive, worthwhile, and achievable vision of the future, widely shared."[72]

One of the concepts I've found useful in developing strategy is a two-dimensional representation of goals. On the one dimension, there are three categories of goals: minimum, realistic, and stretch; and on the other dimension, there are three more categories: routine, problem-solving, and creative. It has been my experience that the more the chosen goals move up and to the right as indicated by the arrow, the more motivational and inspirational the goals become.

Goal-Setting

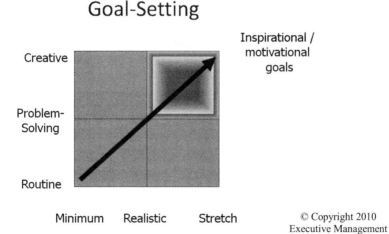

Creative

Problem-Solving

Routine

Inspirational / motivational goals

Minimum   Realistic   Stretch

© Copyright 2010
Executive Management
Systems, Inc.

---

[72] Burt Nanus, *Visionary Leadership* (San Francisco: Jossey-Bass Publishers, 1992) p. 3.

But goal-setting in this phase of strategy development is a combination of art and science.

> *"...while stretch goals can be useful in forcing people to break old rules and do things better, they're worse than useless if they're totally unrealistic, or if the people who have to meet them aren't given the chance to debate them beforehand and take ownership of them."*[73]

It has been my experience that useless stretch goals abound in business. One telltale sign of a useless stretch goal is that they tend to be rewritten when it becomes clear they will be missed by a country mile.

Bridges pave the way to brighter futures. In business, well-crafted strategy is the bridge to a brighter future. Bridges begin with solid footings which support spans.

To build business strategy, Executive Management Systems utilizes two steps:
1. Define businesses' footings: integrity, understanding, concrete growth goals;
2. Construct five spans to link and define a comprehensive business strategy supported by these spans.

Change Leadership – The Fourth Span of Strategy

A vision for the future entails change, a disruption of the status quo. Robert Kennedy said it well when he said, *"Progress is a nice word. But change is its motivator and change has its enemies."* Rosbeth Moss Kanter was a little more colorful when she said, *"Change is like putting lipstick on a bulldog. The bulldog's appearance hasn't improved,*

---

[73] Larry Bossidy and Ram Charan, *Execution: The Discipline of Getting Things Done* (New York: Crown Publishing Group, 2002) p. 37.

but now it's really angry."[74] Herodotus said, *"Illness strikes men when they are exposed to change."* It's been my experience that when it comes to change, it's better (easier) to give than receive. So what's my point? Change leadership is another critical piece to the process of Building Bridges to the Future®.

With the increasing velocity of change, beginning in the '80s, accelerating in the '90s, and reaching warp speed in the new millennium, there has been a lot of attention given to not only change management, but change leadership. Change has to be managed and led not only on the corporate level, but also on the personal level.

William Bridges offers insight on the personal level: *"It isn't the changes that do you in, it's the transitions. They aren't the same thing. Change is situational ... Transition, on the other hand, is psychological."*[75] Bridges defines transition as the neutral stage between endings and new beginnings, and it is a challenging sea to personally navigate. A basic awareness of how change affects individuals is necessary in order to proceed with organizational change.

Price Pritchett cautions: *"Remember the '20-50-30 rule' ... Some 20 percent of the people are 'change-friendly' ... Another 50 percent of the folks sit on the fence ... The remaining 30 percent are the resisters."*[76]

John P. Kotter has done some excellent work on the topic of change leadership. As a result of his experience, he has defined eight steps in the process of leading change[77]:

---

[74] "On Change," *CreatingMinds - Tools, Techniques, Methods, Quotes and Quotations on All Matters Creative* <http://creatingminds.org/quotes/change.html> 11July 2011.

[75] William Bridges, *Managing Transitions: Making the Most of Change* (Cambridge, Massachusetts: Perseus Books Group, 2nd Edition, 2003) p. 3.

[76] Price Pritchett, *Resistance: Moving Beyond the Barriers to Change* (Dallas, TX: Pritchett & Associates, 1997) p. 3.

[77] John P. Kotter, *Leading Change* (Boston: Harvard Business School Press, 1996) p. 21.

- Establishing a sense of urgency
- Creating the guiding coalition
- Developing a vision and strategy
- Communicating the change vision
- Empowering employees for broad-based action
- Generating short-term wins
- Consolidating gains and producing more change
- Anchoring new approaches in the culture

Of interest is Kotter's assertion that *"cultural change comes last, not first."*[78] It has been my experience that organizational culture cannot wait until step #8 to be addressed. It is critical early in the process of building a bridge to the future to address the leadership teams values, ethics and behaviors which shape the organizational culture (reference Chapters Four and Five, especially the graphics on pages 54 and 55).

Mark J. Pastin suggests that an effective key way to address culture is to focus on ethics: *"If you want to initiate basic change in your organization, start discussing ethics."*[79] His logic is clear and compelling: *"Ethics is closer to the surface of an organizational culture than other components (myths, ideologies, and aesthetics). When an organization enforces its ethics, its ground rules come into view."*[80]

It is imperative that organizational culture be engaged via a discussion on ethics early in the strategy development process.

There is one more fundamental point I want to emphasize on the interrelatedness of all of the components of the Building Bridges to the Future® model:

---

[78] Ibid, p. 155.
[79] Mark J. Pastin, Ph. D., "No Ethics, No Change," in *Lessons in Cultural Change,* edited by Philip R. Thiebert (Arlington, Virginia: Public Utilities Reports, Inc. 1994) p. 339.
[80] Ibid, pp. 337-338.

"One of the reasons we have not improved our ability to change organizations is that we still do not understand the relationships among organizational culture, organizational ethics and change. Very simply, organizational culture is a barrier to adaptive change, while adaptive change is impossible without attention to organizational ethics."[81]

Execution – The Fifth Span of Strategy

Once the first four spans of strategy are complete, the packaging of the vision for execution is the important, final span as the bridge to the future is set in place. The final stage – execution – is where the rubber meets the road. With a well-defined, optimistic vision, focused strategy and diligent implementation, corporate and personal transformational results follow. An important step in execution is packaging the vision.

Key outcomes from an organizational intervention by Executive Management Systems include three tangibles – Vision, Focus and Results – on two levels: Corporate and Personal. These outcomes are shown in the following figure, with the outer ring representing the development and implementation of corporate strategy and the inner ring representing the development and implementation of a personal leadership strategy:

---

[81] Ibid, p. 335.

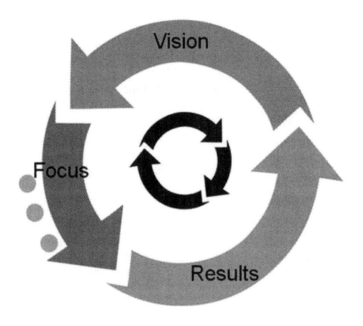

Two levels of transformation: corporate and personal

Both the corporate strategy and the personal leadership strategy are the outcome from the Building Bridges to the Future® process.

Packaging the Vision

Many good visions die due to flawed execution. The execution stage includes deliberate, focused, timely action by the client in all areas identified. It includes pacing, adept sequencing without falling into a plodding, snail's pace implementation. The execution phase may include leadership development, executive coaching, strategic talent management, and succession planning.

"There are different kinds of intellectual challenges. Conceiving a grand idea or broad picture is usually intuitive. Shaping the broad picture into a set of executable actions is analytical, and it's a huge intellectual, emotional and creative challenge."[82]

An important step in accepting the creative challenge is in the packaging of the vision. The shared vision resulting from the building bridges process has to be crisp, clear, motivating, and inspirational. It has to develop the big-picture context of the vision while driving specific direction toward the goals set by the team. It is a focused document, short, to-the-point, visually appealing, no clutter, with ample whitespace for personal notes. It is designed to fly, not sit on the shelf in obscurity.

Clarity of thought and brevity of word are critical in this document. Lack of clarity is an energy-sucking parasite that leads to a shutdown of the temporal lobes.

This document must bear the earmarks, the words, the quotes and the sweat stains of the leadership team on it. This conveys their ownership and evokes strong memories of the teamwork that went into the creation of the shared vision.

The clarity and the energy of this document must engage the organization. This document is a prime mover to create expectations and to create and sustain the necessary momentum to implement the vision. It is visually and intellectually engaging. It builds expectations.

In my work with clients, I have developed visioning documents which meet these criteria and capture the essence of a

---

[82] Larry Bossidy and Ram Charan, *Execution: The Discipline of Getting Things Done* (New York: Crown Publishing Group, 2002), p. 32.

transformational vision ... and they are still alive and well and serving as a roadmap five years after their creation. One client identified the capture and implementation of this vision as a major organizational milestone in their sixty-year history.

Vision – Defining Our Model

In the process of developing a shared vision for the future, it is necessary to define the key visioning concepts in a model which serves as a framework, a delivery vehicle for the vision. Each of these three key concepts – Mission / Goals / Objectives – moves from the big picture to the details, from the general to the specific, and from the long-term to the short-term:

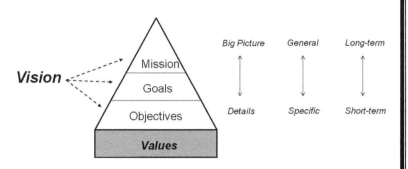

- **Mission** is a straightforward statement of the long-term purpose of the organization and usually serves the organization for 30 years or more.
- **Goals** are more specific and set direction over the next 3-10 years.
- **Objectives** are driven by the goals and include specific actions to be taken and timeframes to be met as goals are achieved.
- **Vision** is a simple statement of direction over the next 3-5 years that is driven by the Mission / Goals / Objectives, which provide the context, the environment, the direction to define the vision. The vision simply summarizes the near-term direction the organization is pursuing to achieve its specific dreams.
- **Values** are the foundational guidelines for the organization's conduct and decision-making. They help to measure the correctness of the course the organization chooses to chart. It is important to include the values in the vision document.

Summary

In developing a bridge to the future, there are five spans of strategy – summarized in the bridge model as **Strategy⁺** – each span representing key, sequential steps. I have touched on each one of these in this chapter:

- Strategic Thinking
- Team Engagement
- Strategy Development
- Change Leadership
- Execution

Let's step back and put Chapter Seven in context. As stated earlier, what makes the Mackinac Bridge succeed is that it is a system of four key, integrated elements. These structural elements – cable anchorages, towers / footings, suspension cables, and the spans / road deck – define the framework for the bridge model: **Values⁺, Relationships⁺, Leadership⁺** and **Strategy⁺**.

As I stated in the introduction, Building Bridges to the Future® is not only a business model, it is a life model. It is the product of all my experiences, both in life and business.

In the final chapter, I will walk you through the elements of the bridge model – **Values⁺, Relationships⁺, Leadership⁺ and Strategy⁺** – on a very personal level, as a life model.

Living Life with Vision

"He that would be a leader must also be a bridge."

– Welsh Proverb

This old Welsh proverb is instructive. Thoughtful reflection on its wisdom yields pretty clear insight.

In travel, bridges point the way to the future, to where we want to be and go. So also must leaders point the way to the future. Bridges carry the load of travel. Leaders help others carry the load of life – opportunities and challenges alike. The character of a bridge stands out and is quite visible – it defines the bridge. So it is with the character of a leader.

Bridges help us go as far as we can see ... and when we get there we can see further. So it is with leaders. It's fitting to close out this book with a chapter on living life with vision ... This chapter could be subtitled: Building Bridges from Here to Eternity.

A short poem from the Mackinac Bridge builder's book comes to mind:

> *Anchored firm in solid rock,*
> > *On Thy foundation let me build –*
> *Strong to bear each strain and shock,*
> > *An arch of dreams and faith fulfilled.*[83]

---

[83]Op. cit., Steinman, p. 70.

Developing a Personal Vision

If we as leaders are to be a bridge to the future, we must practice the disciplines of the model I've set forth in this book on a personal level:

1. Main towers and footings anchored in the bedrock of relationships based on integrity and awareness – truth;
2. Suspension cables – personal leadership – supported by these bedrock relationships;
3. Anchors – a solid set of immovable values; and
4. Specific strategies – spanning the gulf from where we are to where we want to go.

To live life with vision, two areas where leadership is critical are

1. Leadership of one's self; and
2. Leadership in the home – a shared husband-wife leadership.

Before we can develop a shared husband-wife leadership vision, we must start from a strong base of a personal leadership vision. It has been very interesting for me to look back and mine the rich mother lode of perspectives on my life. I'm reminded of the words of Winston Churchill: *"The farther backward you can look, the farther forward you can see."*

Perspectives from Reflection

There are some amazing perspectives that come from reflection, from looking back.

The process of personal reflection is a valuable exercise: "silence, coupled with reflection, a time to contemplate the moment, to assess one's position and progress, to internalize the details and the subtleties of the situation."[84] We need to let the experience of life sink in.

As I look back on my archives of notes, files, and events of my life, what I was reading and thinking and writing at the time, it is instructive for me to review the rich decade I lived from the ages of 35 to 45 (1982 to 1992). I had a lot of moving gears in my life, personally, professionally, as a husband, as a parent of four children, and in community involvement.

This decade in a man's life has been defined by sociologists, psychologists and researchers as the time of mid-life crisis, a time of real upheaval in a man's life. It's a time of change in a man's body and his psyche, a time when he shoulders major responsibilities of career and family.

One of the books I was reading at the time was *Men in Mid-Life Crisis,* by Jim Conway. It is an excellent resource for men approaching mid-life. As a testimony to its timeless value, after more than three decades, it is still in print. The perils of male mid-life crises are real: *"Depression is one of two major emotional feelings prevalent to the man in midlife ... Self-pity is the second predominant theme."*[85]

The second astronaut to set foot on the moon, Colonel Edwin E. "Buzz" Aldrin, Jr., was hit hard by a mid-life crisis: *"My depression forced me, at the age of forty-one, to stop and for the first time examine my life. The circumstances that brought about my study were extreme, but I now look upon this experience as one of the most valuable things I have done. It taught me to live again, at an age when it is very possible to begin anew."*[86]

---

[84] Gloria Gaither, *We Have this Moment* (Waco Texas: Word Books, 1988) p. 11.
[85] Jim Conway, *Men in Mid-Life Crisis* (David C. Cook Publishing Co., 1978) p. 22
[86] Col. Edwin E. "Buzz" Aldrin, Jr., *Return to Earth* (New York: Random, 1973) pp. 308-309.

It is critical that we as men approach that mid-life decade with the right mindset. Anxiety, doubt, and fear build walls which entrap us in the past. Confidence, optimism and hope build bridges which enable us to define, map and choose our future. If we are going to live life with vision, we men need to be especially aware of the challenges we face in mid-life.

> *"If you don't have a positive plan for your future, you may well be putting your relational and physical health at risk ... It may seem that there's no real cost to being aimless, but lack of purpose actually drains energy and life."*[87]

Mid-life can be a time of increased clarity and focus on who we are and what we want to be ... and for me, mid-life was all of that. Some of the key aspects of this rich decade – highlights of my personal vision – include:

1. Developing a written statement of my personal leadership philosophy (discussed previously in Chapter Six)
2. Developing my first extensive Pathfinder list of scriptures (more on this later in the chapter) to chart my course in life
3. Taking the first steps to define a consulting practice
4. Developing and delivering my first leadership development programs – *Meetings that Count* and *Effective Teamwork*
5. Registering the trade name Executive Management Systems
6. Considering and rejecting the launch of a full-time consulting practice (I wanted my kids to know me as they grew up)
7. Considering and rejecting starting in an MBA program (I wanted my kids to know me as they grew up)
8. Teaching numerous adult Bible study classes on a wide variety of topics ... which drove my vision

---

[87] John Trent, *LifeMapping* (Colorado Springs, Colorado: Focus on the Family Publishing, 1994) p. 17.

9. Shifting my career focus from system operations to marketing and public relations

That decade was a rich and productive time as I developed real clarity and a sharp focus on my personal vision. It absolutely and fundamentally defined the next twenty years of my life. My personal life vision developed during this decade, and my subsequent experience for the two most recent decades of my life drive home the point in this book's title and subtitle – *Building Bridges: Today's Decisions – Gateway to Your Future.*

Developing a Shared Vision

Let's shift gears and talk about shared husband-wife leadership. One of the most rewarding things I've ever done is to be a parent. As a recently-minted grandparent, it's time for me to review the basics.

To put this story in context, I have to back up nearly three decades. My wife and I had set a goal in 1984 that we were going to take the kids to Disney Land in 1987. In 1985, I had an older, wiser business associate ask me, *"Mel, how old is your oldest? By the time he's 10, you had better start spending a lot of time with him and the rest of the family. If you don't, soon he'll be 15 – with his friends and all kinds of activities – and he won't want to spend time with you and the family."*

Gary Smalley first published *The Key to Your Child's Heart* in 1983, which we found very helpful in raising a family. One of the highlights I recall was the research done on what constitutes a close family. They found two factors: families that spent a lot of time together camping and/or running a family business.

As we developed our vision and dreams for our family, my wife and I chose the camping route ... which brings us full circle in this book. The motor home we purchased in 1987 was the vehicle that introduced us to the Mackinac Bridge in 1993.

Renewed Personal Vision

At a time when many men go through a mid-life crisis, I was fortunate to be defining a renewed strategy for personal growth and development. The year 1987 was pivotal. I celebrated my fortieth birthday. I bought a motor home and took a 3½-week trip with family. I moved into a different career path, from power system operations to an executive position in marketing and public relations.

The first year we had that motor home – 1987 – we spent 42 nights in it, on a variety of trips. Our three sons were aged 10, 8, and 6 and our daughter was 3. Twenty-five of the 42 nights were spent on that 3½-week trip, which took us from North Dakota to California and back.

It was a great family bonding experience. We hit eight national parks and Disney Land. It was a trip that was part of the vision my wife and I developed as we raised our family, and it was a trip that had been in our plans for several years. That memorable trip is still a highlight of our most cherished family memories. In 1988, we took a 2½-week motor home trip to Disney World.

In 1989, *Secret Choices* was published. Subtitled *Personal Decisions That Affect Your Marriage*, it was written by two marriage counselors, Ed Wheat, M.D. and Gloria Okes Perkins. The book zeroed in on the question, "In what direction is your marriage headed?" The back cover of the book included a statement which summarized the book well:

> *"Life is a series of choices, most of them so small we scarcely realize that we're making them. Or why. Sometimes we call*

them 'reactions' and disclaim any responsibility for them, not recognizing that reactions are choices, too. We seldom give thought to where these small, secret choices are taking us and whether we want to go there ..."

This book had an impact on us ... as did another by Chuck Swindoll, given to me by my brother-in-law at Christmas, 1989: *Living Above the Level of Mediocrity.* Swindoll wrote in the introduction:

"I'm convinced that achieving one's full potential is still a goal worth striving for ... And so, my fellow eagle, we're off! And by the time we've completed this flight, we shall be more committed than ever to a life of excellence. We'll be so encouraged that it's doubtful we can ever be satisfied living anywhere near the level of mediocrity again. But then why should we? That's where life gets dull, drab, predictable, and tiring. Or perhaps the most descriptive word is boring, a direct result of low aim. Let's lift our sights and aim so high that we start doing the thing God made us for: soaring."[88]

Charting a Course for Our Children

There was a third very useful book[89] that I was introduced to in the mid-'80s by Dallas Theological Seminary in a magazine article *"In Our Steps."*[90]

Two key premises of that article and book are that:

---

[88] Charles R. Swindoll, *Living Above the Level of Mediocrity* (Waco, Texas: Word Books Publisher, 1987) p. 13.
[89] *How to Raise Confident Children* by Richard L. Strauss (Grand Rapids, MI: Baker Book House, 1984)
[90] *Kindred Spirit* (published quarterly by Dallas Theological Seminary, Dallas, Texas, 75204) Summer, 1985. Vol. 9 No. 2, p. 16.

1. "God gives parents to children to help build the qualities into them that will prepare them for a most useful and satisfying life."

2. "Discipline, contrary to popular opinion, is far more than correction. It is charting a course for our children, guiding them along that course, and firmly but lovingly bringing them back to that course when they stray."

Developing Our Shared Vision

Taken together, these three books – coupled with twenty years of shared life experiences in marriage – gave us fresh motivation and insightful methodologies for living life with a renewed sense of vision.

From the start, our marriage was defined by deeply held and shared personal convictions, our values, our life view. From the "get-go," our vision for married life together was focused on Solomon's wisdom in Proverbs 3:5-6 (NLT):

> [5] Trust in the Lord with all your heart;
> do not depend on your own understanding.
> [6] Seek his will in all you do,
> and he will show you which path to take.

In 1990, we developed our shared vision. It was updated over the next decade as our children moved into adulthood. Now with four grandchildren, soon to be six, it needs another update. Three years ago, we purchased a lake cabin as insurance that our grandchildren will stay close enough to us for our influence to rub off.

A shared vision is a very personal thing. I include ours here, because one of the most important bridges I'll build with my wife stretches from here to eternity. In my opinion, that's the essence of living life with vision.

Our Shared Vision

October 6, 1990
Revised 9-5-91 / 4-12-92 / 3-8-98 / 3-30-98

What is Most Important in Our Life:

To bring out the best character,
talents, abilities, and qualities
in each other
and in our children
to the glory of God.

Our Purpose Statement for Our Shared Life:

To live an abundant life,
to model Godly character and behavior,
and become the individuals that God meant us to be.

OUR PRIORITIES

1. To become the persons that God intended us to be:

    a. To live an abundant life;
    b. To model Godly character and behavior; and
    c. To use our spiritual gifts to the glory of God.

2. To rise well above the "level of mediocrity" with our attitudes and behavior.

3. To live life without regrets.

4. Together, to build strong habit patterns to affirm our love for:

   a. Life;
   b. Each other;
   c. Our children;
   d. Our neighbors/fellow man; and
   e. Our God.

5. Be successful parents by:

   a. Becoming the persons that God intended us to be; and
   b. Staying close enough to our kids for it to rub off.

6. Enjoy life in the present:

   a. Live each day with a healthy balance, focusing on the priorities (and not "the urgent");
   b. Develop rich memories as we go – today;
   c. Face the future with optimism; and
   d. Look back to yesterday with gratefulness.

Bible Promises:

Romans 14:19 (NASB) –

> *"So then let us pursue the things*
> *which make for peace*
> *and the building up*
> *of one another."*

I Thessalonians 5:11 (NASB) –

> *"Therefore encourage one another,*
> *and build up one another,*
> *just as you also are doing."*

I Thessalonians 5:16-18 (NASB) –

"Rejoice always;
Pray without ceasing;
in everything give thanks;
for this is God's will for you
in Christ Jesus..."

Philippians 4:8 (NASB) –

"Finally, brethren, whatever is true,
whatever is honorable,
whatever is right,
whatever is pure,
whatever is lovely,
whatever is of good repute,
if there is any excellence and
if anything worthy of praise,
let your mind dwell on these things."

Philippians 2:1-4 (NASB) –

"If therefore there is any encouragement
in Christ,
if any consolation of love,
if there is any fellowship of the Spirit,
if any affection and compassion,
make my joy complete
by being of the same mind,
maintaining the same love, united in spirit,
intent on one purpose.

Do nothing from selfishness or empty conceit,
but with humility of mind,
let each of you regard one another

as more important than himself;
do not merely look out
for your own personal interests,
but also for the interests of others."

CHILDREN: CHARTING A COURSE[91]

1. Lead them to a saving knowledge of Jesus Christ;

2. Lead them to a total commitment of their lives to Christ;

3. Build the Word of God into their lives;

4. Teach them prompt and cheerful obedience and respect for authority;

5. Teach them self discipline;

6. Teach them to accept responsibility;

7. Teach them the basic traits of Christian character.

---

[91] Excerpted from the article "In Our Steps" from *Kindred Spirit* (Dallas Theological Seminary, Dallas, Texas). Vol. 9 No. 2 (Summer, 1985) p. 16.

YOUNG ADULTS – CHARTING the TRANSITION to ADULTHOOD
(2-26-98, 9-24-98, 2-11-99, 8-21-99, 1-2-00)

To coach, encourage, nurture, and enable our children:

1. To live/walk by faith:

    a. By our example as parents
    b. By noting biblical examples of faith
    c. By identifying examples of faith around us
    d. By seeking ways to exhibit faith

2. To make timely decisions with wisdom and confidence

3. To develop a world view from a Christian perspective:

    a. Welcoming learning
    b. Remembering that all truth is God's truth
    c. Never forgetting that "the fear of the Lord is the beginning of wisdom"

4. To take personal responsibility for life choices:

    a. Choice of university
    b. Field of study
    c. Timely completion of education (bachelor's in four years)
    d. Financial accountability/wisdom
    e. Career field
    f. Choice of friends
    g. Spiritual walk
    h. Choice of mate

5. To continue to pursue learning as a lifelong venture:

   a. Spiritual
   b. Mental
   c. Social
   d. Emotional
   e. Financial
   f. Professional

6. To maintain sexual purity as a family:

   a. Thought life
   b. Verbal/conversation
   c. Reading material
   d. Movies, video, television

7. To take life a day at a time:

   a. Trusting God each step of the way
   b. Taking small steps of faith
   c. Allowing God to develop us along the way

8. Learn from the past ... Live in the present ... Plan for the future ...

9. To choose each day to live differently by implementing four strategies to confront the world system[92]:

   a. **Vision** – see above and beyond the majority and "envision what most people would miss"

   b. **Determination** – "inner fortitude, strength of character, being disciplined to remain consistent,

---

[92] Op. cit., Swindoll, *Living Above the Level of Mediocrity*, pp. 80-81.

strong, and diligent regardless of the odds or the demands"

c. **Priorities** – "choosing first things first, doing essential things in the order of importance, bypassing the incidentals"

d. **Accountability** – "answering the hard questions, being closely in touch with a few individuals rather than living like an isolated Lone Ranger"

Life Vision Benchmarking

A year and a half after writing this shared vision, my wife and I had an opportunity to benchmark our shared vision against another construct, and consider the balance and completeness of our vision from another perspective.

Life Span[93]

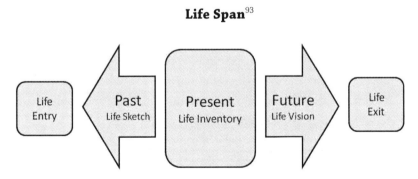

In itself, this visual is instructive, since it captures the essence of a very useful framework for living life from the perspective of personal vision. We have "benchmarked" our shared vision against other constructs over the years, and refined our focus as we felt

---

[93] From a presentation by Dr. Ramesh Richard, May 2, 1992: *Life Span – Shaping Your Life's Direction.* Used with permission.

necessary. These adjustments are reflected in the numerous revision dates on the shared vision.

Reflection on Living Life with Vision

After having lived out this shared vision for over twenty years, it is instructive to look back and reflect on some of the key life lessons learned. Four stand out: (1) the role of pathfinder Bible verses; (2) expanding the shared vision when our children matured into young adults and began leaving the nest; and (3) living life with vision includes walking by faith; and (4) the impact on my children.

Pathfinder Verses

One of the tools I've always used to set my personal gyro for life navigation is what I call my "pathfinder list." It is a list of my favorite scripture passages that help me choose my direction.

The pathfinders have been a very important military unit of strategic value in military operations. During the D-Day operations in WWII, for example, special pathfinder teams were parachuted in ahead of the inland airborne assault in June 1944 at Normandy. Their role was to set up radio beacons to eliminate navigational error for the planes carrying the paratroopers to their drop zones. In the Viet Nam conflict, pathfinders would go in ahead of major airborne assaults to guide helicopter landing operations in the thick jungles of Southeast Asia.

So it is with my pathfinder Bible verses. They help me set my direction. King David said in Psalm 119:105 (NLT):

Your word is a lamp to guide my feet and a light for my path.

These pathfinder verses function like a Contac capsule or a medicinal "patch" by continually releasing God's wisdom into my bloodstream and psyche while I navigate the challenges of life. These very pathfinder verses – God's truth – can be woven into the fabric of our children's lives.

This point was forcefully driven home to me recently. In 1990, one of the key motor home trips we took as a family was from Fargo to Vancouver for my folks' fiftieth wedding anniversary. On the way out we stopped in Glacier National Park. One beautiful Sunday morning my wife and I took a hike up the mountain side with our four children – aged 13, 11, 9 and 6 – to enjoy God's creation and a time of worship in the wonderful ampitheater of the Rocky Mountains.

As we travelled down the highway, each of the kids took turns reading assigned scriptures from the Psalms. My eldest son was assigned Psalm 104 and was asked to summarize the chapter in our discussion travelling down the highway.

Nearly twenty years later, in 2009, I was hunting elk in the Rocky Mountains with my eldest son. We took many awe-inspiring pictures which he summarized and published in a book entitled *An Elk Hunting Adventure: The Bob Marshall Wilderness* (© 2009, Joel Nelson). On the title page, he included three verses selected from the Psalms:

Psalm 19:1 (NIV)

The heavens declare the glory of God; the skies proclaim the work of his hands.

Psalm 104:10 (NIV)

You make springs pour water into the ravines, so streams gush down from the mountains

Psalm 104:24 (NIV)

O Lord, what a variety of things you have made! In wisdom you have made them all. The earth is full of your creatures.

After I got the book, one night I was reviewing some old files of our travels as a family. I ran across the list of assigned scriptures for our family worship after that 1990 hike on the mountain. It was then I realized the connection between the two travel memories nearly 20 years apart. I have many other good memories of how God's Word has been woven into the lives of my children.

Young Adults

The second life perspective after living this vision for twenty years is that our family went through a major transition as our children moved from youths to young adults as they took on the college years. This section of the shared vision reflects that transition – a transition not only in their lives but a transition in our role as parents:

To coach, encourage, nurture, and enable our children:

1. *To live/walk by faith*
2. *To make timely decisions with wisdom & confidence*
3. *To develop a world view from a Christian perspective*
4. *To take personal responsibility for life choices*
5. *To continue to pursue learning as a lifelong venture*
6. *To maintain sexual purity as a family*
7. *To take life a day at a time*

8. *Learn from the past ... Live in the present ... Plan for the future; and*
9. *To choose each day to live differently by implementing four strategies to confront the world system – vision, determination, priorities, and accountability*

My perspective? A shared vision has different chapters to it, as a husband and wife move through life together. The basics remain in place, and some chapters of the shared vision become useful benchmarks and reminders of where a couple has been.

Game-Changing Transitions

The third life perspective after living this vision for twenty years is that we can weather difficult life circumstances, game-changing transitions, if we live life with vision.

During Thanksgiving of 1999, our eldest son said to me, "You know, you and Mom have had things pretty good. Are you really walking by faith?" That was a great conversation. Little did I know it would be a game-changer. As I reflected on that conversation over the next month, through Christmas and into the New Year, I wrote in my journal and updated our shared vision on January 2, 2000, to include this statement:

To live/walk by faith:

> *By our example as parents;*
> *By noting biblical examples of faith;*
> *By identifying examples of faith around us; and*
> *By seeking ways to exhibit faith.*

Ten days after adding this goal to our shared vision, my executive position was eliminated. Gone. We truly went from trusting a corporation for our paycheck to trusting God. Thus started the transition that I spoke of in Chapter One.

Had we not gone through that transition, this book would never have been written. I would likely have gone to my grave with a lot of my music still in me. Living life with vision and walking by faith have combined to make the last decade one of the richest in my life.

Impact on My Children

Living out this shared vision with my wife over the last twenty years has had a significant impact on my children, on who they are, on what they've become, and where they are headed in life. We wanted to help each of our children develop to the fullest of their potential, and our shared vision reflects that.

Of my four children, I've mentioned elsewhere in this book each of my three sons, but not my daughter Annie. She was the youngest, growing up with three older brothers. When she was married, her brothers were on the platform with her. When the pastor asked, *"Who gives this woman to be married to this man?"*, I had to answer, *"Her mother, her brothers, and I"* ... which was received by the guests and friends with chuckles and smiles. It was true. These four children were family ... with all of the privileges and responsibilities which that entails.

As the youngest, with three older brothers, one might expect that she would be overshadowed by them. Not at all. As a young girl, she projected confidence and insight. When she spoke, her brothers listened. She was very relational. She could size up a situation quickly and take action. We recognized these talents early and sought to reinforce them. She is also a very good deer hunter.

She was in a pharmacy program, but decided that she would rather be with people, where there was action, so she chose to transfer to nursing. Today as an emergency room nurse, she is in charge of training new nurses coming into the ER. Her work is a good, close fit with her talents and temperament.

She recently received a prestigious award for her work in the ER, "The Lamp of Knowledge Award." The nomination her supervisor sent in for the award called out Annie's personal qualities of "commitment," "role model," "loves to learn," "detail-oriented," "organized," and "every bit the professional." The nomination also included the following endorsement:

> *"Annie is not only a unit educator but she is also charge nurse, triage nurse, One Call nurse, TAG nurse and patient care nurse. She is aware that in these roles it is essential that she model the highest level of nursing care because she is working with the same people that she is teaching. She is aware that it is essential that she puts theory into practice on an every day, every situation, no exception basis. She is aware that others are watching her. She is aware that she will be asked questions, will be asked to teach, no matter which hat she is wearing on any particular day. Annie is aware of all this and has taken the challenge displaying grace, patience, calmness and kindness."*

> *"Annie believes in lifelong learning. She enjoys it. She also enjoys teaching others and it shows. It shows in her attitude, her smile, her openness, her approachability. It shows in her dedication and her passion for nursing. She takes pride in watching others become more confident, more knowledgeable and then passing that knowledge on to their coworkers, patients and families. She does hold the Lamp of Knowledge. She holds it high, for herself and for those around her."*

We believe that the environment we created in the home with our shared vision allowed each of our children to develop and maximize their talent and abilities ... and we see irrefutable evidence of that in who they have become and the life choices they are making.

Perspective

John Ortberg has drawn some interesting life perspectives from the game of Monopoly. One of these lessons is on keeping score. Key questions include, *"How do we learn to keep score?"* and *"From whom do we learn to keep score?"* The overarching caution here is that we need to be very careful in choosing what determines our sense of worth. God's scoring system in life is not extrinsic. It's not about comparison, competition, and climbing to the top. It is intrinsic. It's about who we are ... It is not about what we have.[94]

Ortberg's greatest lesson from Monopoly is captured in the title of his book: *"When the game is over, it all goes back in the box."*

Let's simplify this. Life has an entry point, just like any business startup. Good entrepreneurs know that a good business startup also includes an exit plan.

The same is true when we build our life bridge.

Our
Life
Bridge

Birth   Death

---

[94] John Ortberg. *When the Game Is Over, It All Goes Back in the Box* (Grand Rapids: Zondervan, 2007).

At the end of life, what legacy do we leave? Does our bridge continue beyond death? What's your exit plan?

It is this legacy point of view that is reflected in our shared vision as husband and wife. The process of developing a shared vision and living life with vision defines the legacy we will leave to our children and grandchildren.

A Grandfather's Legacy

Four years ago, my father-in-law passed away. When my son David spoke at his funeral, he defined the kind of legacy we would like to leave our children and grandchildren:

"It's difficult coming up with something to say at a funeral for someone you love. Where do you start? With the memories you had with them? What they were like? What they passed on to you? A legacy?"

"I'll start with my picture of Grampa. I knew Grampa during the autumn of his life – not as a child or young man. But I imagine Grampa has been the same throughout his life – a man of few words, a quiet man who enjoyed being around others immensely even if he didn't talk much, someone who found great pleasure in the simpler things in life – a drive through lake country, a good Louis L'Amour book, a Diet Coke, his beloved auction sales, and a sit-down meal with someone he cared about. Many of these traits he passed on to others in this room – my Uncle Dick and myself come quickly to mind."

"It was often sacred being around Grampa; he was a direct link to our past, our roots, our ancestors – both Swedish and Italian. Driving to the family farm or the cemetery with him was my most palpable link to his time and the generations that came before him.

Grampa, as well as his siblings, has done an incredible job researching and preserving the past, capturing it for his children and grandchildren."

"Being able to verbally articulate love to those in your family is tricky. I imagine this is the case in most families. One Christmas during my college years, I attempted to do this. Grampa had had one of his previous brushes with death, and I knew Grampa could be gone at any time. I mustered up the courage to tell Grampa something like this, '*Grampa, I'm really glad you're here with us this year. You're a very special person to me. Some of my best memories in life have been with you, and I really love you'.*"

"Grampa had not seen it coming. He squirmed a little and said, '*Oh, David … you're a good boy.'* That was all."

"I could tell he was uncomfortable with my forthrightness, and I wasn't going to say anything else. I had said what I wanted to say, and he received it. I had only verbally acknowledged what we already knew existed without words. I don't know how many people have had a conversation like this with Donald, but I do know a great deal of care and love was flowing to and from this quiet man, whether they were made visible by words or not."

"I also don't know how much Grampa was able to directly express his love with words during his lifetime to those closest to him, but I do know that during those last agonizing weeks he woke up from his confusion and had a window of lucid thought. During this brief moment, he communicated clear words of love for his family, his children. I am very glad that quiet Grampa found his words – it means something to all of us. Perhaps words of love are necessary, acting as a visible receipt that some mutual transaction has really taken place, and you can hold onto that receipt without a doubt."

"I'll finish this with one of my most special memories with Grampa. It was Labor Day weekend during one of my high school years. I had finished the first week of school; I was wound up as could be – stressed and anxious. Grampa and I were going to be spending the three-day weekend at Crane Lake. It was a much-needed break from my busy summer and the first week of class. I met up with him in Aber. Harvest was going on. As we drove, I got Grampa telling me about growing up in the '20s and '30s. I tried to imagine the landscape without paved roads, modern cars, and combines. He said they had little money and possessions growing up, but he didn't know any better and had as happy a childhood as anyone could have. He carried this attitude with him throughout his life, getting great joy from very little."

"We did a lot that weekend. We ate at his favorite places. I even got him out fishing in the boat on a serene Saturday evening. We spent most of Sunday morning driving his white Cadillac. He took me for brunch at a cafe that I had never been to nor want to find again; not because I did not like it, but because it holds a place in my heart."

"On the way back, we decided to drive where we wanted to – no directions, just turn where we felt like it. There was a tape playing in the car – a compilation of songs from Patsy Cline and Willie to Benny Goodman and Glenn Miller. We drove for what seemed to be hours, and, at the same time, no time at all. No words between us, listening to the music, looking at the colorful leaves on this crisp autumn morning."

"As simple and ordinary as this sounds, I believe this drive was one of my most real glimpses of heaven on this side of the grave. Grampa had been here though before, not on these roads, but in this place. And now I was here with him – together."

"Life is filled with trial and suffering, but it is also filled with good times and these brief moments in our lives where everything is right and you sense a deep communion with nature, with others, with God. This was one such moment – and I was with Grampa".

"As satisfying as this moment was, I believe it is only a shadow, a hint, of the eternal joy that Grampa is experiencing right now with his Maker. My mom is right to say that Grampa no longer needs his hearing aids and can clearly hear us say we love you and will miss you for the time being."

Living Life with a Long Term Perspective

Viktor Frankl said, *"It is a peculiarity of man that he can only live by looking to the future."*[95] King Solomon said in his book Ecclesiastes that God has put eternity in man's heart:

> *Yet God has made everything beautiful for its own time. He has planted eternity in the human heart.*
>
> — Ecclesiastes 3:11 (NLT)

The logical conclusion we must draw from this is that we'd better plan ahead.

Contrast Solomon's wisdom with man's perspective, as captured in John Denver's song "Sweet Surrender." It's a song about wandering aimlessly, and in a token way, seeking purpose and meaning, but not as a serious endeavor. It's a song about living "without care" as fish and birds do.

Man has a soul. Birds and fish do not. Man will live in eternity ... but birds and fish won't. ... So we of the human race had better plan

---

[95] Viktor E. Frankl, *Man's Search for Meaning* (New York: Simon & Schuster, 1984) p. 81.

ahead. When life is over, and it "all goes back in the box" – including us – our soul lives on for eternity.

This is why life must be lived with purpose, direction ... and vision.

Birth   Our
Life-Bridge   Death   Eternity

Conclusion

I want to conclude this chapter where we started, with that old Welsh proverb: *"He that would be a leader must also be a bridge."*

A life lived without vision is like a bridge to nowhere. Are you going to live your life with vision, giving serious consideration to the legacy you leave?

One of the interesting exercises for us to gain perspective is to write our epitaph. On the humorous side, there are some funny epitaphs on gravestones across our fair land. One of my friends has a book of humorous epitaphs. One which captures the humor of its owner reads simply, *"I told you I was sick."*

Personally, I would like something with a little more substance as my epitaph:

> *"He built bridges to the future for his clients ...*
> *and a bridge to eternity for his family."*

Epilogue

During the course of writing this book, I gave serious consideration to rearranging the contents of the book to put the business aspects first, followed by the personal, autobiographical elements, with some content moved to the appendix. In fact, this was driven home in a recent conversation I had with a business leader whom I respect very much. But I concluded ultimately that I could not separate the autobiographical elements from the development of the model. They are so interlinked – like strands of DNA – that to pull them apart would do damage to both. He agreed and his suggestion was to strengthen the transitions between the various chapters of the book so that the reader could follow the logic and the interconnectedness of the entire content.

This approach was reinforced by my editor whom I respect and who has known me personally and professionally over the last 20 years. He had seen my labor firsthand to tell this story. He sees it as a unified whole. Two other professionals also lent support to this approach.

I had a recent opportunity to present the Building Bridges to the Future® model to a class of doctoral students in organizational leadership. We talked about how the net sum of personal behaviors and values creates the culture of the organization. The course instructor observed that "You cannot do just one piece … You cannot do the organizational piece without the personal piece."

One of my executive clients, for whom I have worked on a variety of engagements, echoed this when he said, "I've read a lot of business books. From a business standpoint, the wisdom in this book is in the personal piece, the values piece."

These sentiments reinforce the conviction I had as I wrote this book: I wanted to tell the story of how I developed the Building Bridges to the Future® model. To attempt to do so without the very personal autobiographical elements would leave a very important part of the story untold.

I would like to add one final thought. In the course of my work in recent years, I have been asked if I can separate my personal faith from my business. I cannot. Who I am and what I believe – my personal values, ethics and perspective – are inseparably linked with the way I see and do business ... and I believe that I have made a compelling argument for that approach to both life and business. You be the judge. Would you agree?

Bibliography / Works Cited

"About the Air Force: Our Values - Airforce.com." *United States Air Force - Airforce.com.* Web. 29 Apr. 2010. <http://www.airforce.com/learn-about/our-values/>.

"About the Memorial: Quick Facts." Web. 29 Apr. 2010. *United States Air Force Memorial – Air Force Memorial.org* <http://www.airforcememorial.org/memorial/facts.asp>.

"*Akashi Kaikyō Bridge.*" Wikipedia, the Free Encyclopedia. Web. 19 July 2008. <http://en.wikipedia.org/wiki/Akashi_Kaikyo_Bridge>.

Aldrin, Col. Edwin E. "Buzz" Jr. *Return to Earth.* New York: Random, 1973.

Bennis, Warren & Nanus, Burt. Leaders: *The Strategies for Taking Charge.* New York: Harper & Row, Publishers, Inc., 1985.

Bossidy, Larry and Charan, Ram. *Execution: The Discipline of Getting Things Done.* New York, NY: Crown Business, 2002.

"*Bridge Celebration.*" Unity Bridge. Web. 30 July 2011. <http://yabusbridge.blogspot.com/2009/07/bridge-celebration.html>.

Brady, Christopher, and Orrin Woodward. *Launching a Leadership Revolution: Mastering the Five Levels of Influence.* New York, NY: Business Plus, 2005. Print.

"*Bridge Reviews Imperfect.*" The Forum [Fargo] 15 Nov. 2007. Print.

Bridges, William. *Managing Transitions: Making the Most of Change.* Cambridge, Massachusetts: Perseus Books Group, 2nd Edition, 2003.

Butler, John & Imelda and Nelson, Melvin D. *Business Model Innovation: Proven Strategies That Actually Work.* Sevierville, TN: Insight Publishing, 2010.

Buzzell, Dr. Sid, General Editor. *The Leadership Bible: Leadership Principles from God's Word.* Grand Rapids, MI: Zondervan Publishing House, 1998.

"Charles Reade Famous Quote about Act, Habit, Reap, Sow, Thought | Quotes Daddy." *1,000,000 Famous Quotes and Quotations | QuotesDaddy.* Web. 2 June 2011. <http://www.quotesdaddy.com/quote/159776/charles-reade/sow-a-thought-and-you-reap-an-act-sow-an-act-and-you>.

Clancy, Tom with Franks, General Fred Jr. (Ret.), *Into the Storm: A Study in Command.* New York: G.P. Putnam's Sons, 1997.

Collins, James C. & Porras, Jerry I. *Built to Last: Successful Habits of Visionary Companies*, HarperCollins Publishers, Inc., New York, 2002.

Conway, Jim. *Men in Mid-Life Crisis.* David C. Cook Publishing Co., 1978.

Covey, Stephen R. *The 7 Habits of Highly Effective People.* New York: Simon & Schuster, 1989.

de Vries, Manfred Kets *The Leader on the Couch*, John Wiley & Sons, Ltd., West Sussex, England, 2006.

Drakeford, John. The *Awesome Power of the Listening Ear*. Waco, Texas: Word Books, 1967.

Essential Skills of Communicating. Omaha, Nebraska: Vital Learning, 2010.

"Experts: Bridge Policy Better." The Forum [Fargo] 14 Nov. 2007. Print.

"For the Want of a Nail ... by Benjamin Franklin." Web. 2 June 2011. <http://www.quotedb.com/quotes/464>.

Fornes, Mike. *Images of America: Mackinac Bridge*. Chicago: Arcadia Publishing, 2007.

Frankl, Viktor E. *Man's Search for Meaning*. New York: Simon & Schuster, 1984.

Gaither, Gloria. *We Have this Moment*. Waco, Texas: Word Books, 1988.

Galford, Robert and Drapeau, Anne Seibold. *The Trusted Leader*, Free Press, New York, 2002.

Goleman, Daniel, Boyatzis, Richard, and McKee, Annie. *"Primal Leadership: Learning to Lead with Emotional Intelligence."* Boston: Harvard Business School Press, 2002.

Hubbard, Freeman H. *The Train that Never Came Back*. New York: McGraw-Hill Book Company, Inc., 1952) *"The Broken Lantern"*.

Hybels, Bill. *The Power of a Whisper: Hearing God, Having the Guts to Respond*. Grand Rapids: Zondervan, 2010. Print.

"In Our Steps," Kindred Spirit (published quarterly by Dallas Theological Seminary, Dallas) Summer, 1985. Vol. 9 No. 2.

"Kate Shelley." Quarry Depot. Web. 14 Feb. 2011. <http://quarrydepot.com/ks.html>.

Kotter, John P. *Leading Change.* Boston: Harvard Business School Press, 1996.

Kouzes, James M. and Posner, Barry Z. *The Leadership Challenge,* 3rd edition. New York, NY: John Wiley & Sons, Inc., 2002.

Kram, K.E *"Phases of the Mentor Relationship,"* Academy of Management Journal, 26 (1983).

Kublai Khan. (n.d.). BrainyQuote.com. Retrieved July 30, 2011, from *BrainyQuote.com* Web site: http://www.brainyquote.com /quotes/quotes/k/kublaikhan262411.html

Leadership and the Structure of Trust, Paul R. Lawrence and Robert Porter Lynch. The European Business Review, May-June 2011.

Lynn, Adele B. *The Emotional Intelligence Activity Book.* American Management Association: New York, 2002.

"MDOT - David B. Steinman (1887-1961)." *SOM - State of Michigan.* Web. June-July 2008. <http://www.michigan.gov/mdot/0,1607,7-151-9620_11154_41535-126386--,00.html>.

Modern Marvels: The Mackinac Bridge. The History Channel, 2001. DVD.

Nanus, Burt. *Visionary Leadership.* San Francisco: Jossey-Bass Publishers, 1992.

"New River Gorge Bridge." Wikipedia, the Free Encyclopedia. Web. 19 July 2008.
<http://en.wikipedia.org/wiki/New_River_Gorge_Bridge>

O'Leary, Jeffrey. *The Centurion Principles: Battlefield Lessons for Frontline Leaders.* Nashville: Thomas Nelson, 2004. Print.

"On Change." CreatingMinds - Tools, Techniques, Methods, Quotes and Quotations on All Matters Creative. Web. 11 July 2011.
<http://creatingminds.org/quotes/change.html>.

Ortberg, John. *When the Game Is Over, It All Goes Back in the Box.* Grand Rapids: Zondervan, 2007.

Owen, James P. *Cowboy Ethics: What Wall Street Can Learn from the Code of the West,* Ketchum, ID: Stoecklein Publishing & Photography, 2005.

Pastin, Mark J. Ph. D. *"No Ethics, No Change," in Lessons in Cultural Change,* edited by Philip R. Thiebert. Arlington, Virginia: Public Utilities Reports, Inc. 1994.

Personal Listening Profile: Melvin D. Nelson, January 6, 2004. Inscape Publishing, Version 1.1 (C) 2003. Print.

Peters, Thomas J. and Waterman, Robert H. Jr. *In Search of Excellence.* New York: Harper & Row, 1982.

Phillips-Jones, L. *The New Mentors & Protégés.* Grass Valley, CA: Coalition of Counseling Centers 1997.

Pritchett, *Price. Resistance: Moving Beyond the Barriers to Change.* Dallas, TX: Pritchett & Associates, 1996. Print.

Pritchett, Price. *The Ethics of Excellence.* Dallas, TX: Pritchett & Associates, 1997. Print.

Richard, Dr. Ramesh. *Life Span – Shaping Your Life's Direction.* From a presentation May 2, 1992.

Rockwell, Norman. *"My Adventures As an Illustrator,"* ed. T. Rockwell, Saturday Evening Post CCXXXIX 24 Sept.1966.

Rosser, Manda K. *"Chief Executive Officers: Their Mentoring Relationships,"* Ph.D. dissertation, Texas A&M University, December 2004.

Steinman, David B. and Nevill, John T. *Miracle Bridge at Mackinac.* Grand Rapids: Wm. B. Eerdmans Publishing Co., 1957.

Strauss. Richard L. *How to Raise Confident Children* Grand Rapids: Baker Book House, 1984.

Sull, Donald N. *"Why Good Companies Go Bad,"* in Harvard Business Review on Culture and Change,. Boston: Harvard Business School Publishing, 2002.

Swindoll, Charles R. David: *A Man of Passion and Destiny*, Word Publishing, Inc. Dallas, Texas, 1997.

Swindoll, Charles R. Living *Above the Level of Mediocrity.* Waco, Texas: Word Books Publisher, 1987.

Team Dimensions Profile Group Report. July 28, 2011. Inscape Publishing, Version 2.0 ©2005. Print.

The Builders: Marvels of Engineering. Washington, DC: National Geographic Society, 1992. Print.

Trent, John. *LifeMapping.* Colorado Springs, Colorado: Focus on the Family Publishing, 1994.

"Value." Dictionary and Thesaurus - Merriam-Webster Online. Web. 29 Apr. 2010. <http://www.merriam-webster.com/dictionary/value>.

"Value." Dictionary and Thesaurus - Merriam-Webster Online. Web. 29 Apr. 2010. <http://www.merriam-webster.com/thesaurus/value>.

"Value." Wikipedia, the Free Encyclopedia. Web. 29 Apr. 2010. <http://en.wikipedia.org/wiki/Value>.

Von Oech, Roger. *A Kick in the Seat of the Pants: Using Your Explorer, Artist, Judge and Warrior to Be More Creative.* New York, NY: Perennial Library, 1986. Print.

Watson, Thomas J. *A Business and its Beliefs,* as quoted by James C. Collins, Built to Last.

"What Is Beliefs? Definition and Meaning." BusinessDictionary.com - Online Business Dictionary. Web. 29 Apr. 2010. <http://www.businessdictionary.com/definition/beliefs.html>.

"What Is Culture? Definition and Meaning." BusinessDictionary.com - Online Business Dictionary. Web. 29 Apr. 2010. <http://www.businessdictionary.com/definition/culture.html>.

"What Is Organizational Culture? Definition and Meaning." BusinessDictionary.com - Online Business Dictionary. Web. 29 Apr. 2010.
<http://www.businessdictionary.com/definition/organizational-culture.html>.

"What Is Values? Definition and Meaning." BusinessDictionary.com - Online Business Dictionary. Web. 29 Apr. 2010.
<http://www.businessdictionary.com/definition/values.html>.

Zenger, John H. & Folkman, Joseph R. *The Extraordinary Leader: Turning Good Managers into Great Leaders*, McGraw Hill, New York, 2009.

"Zhao Xiao." Web. 21 Aug. 2010.
<Http://www.willowcreek.com/events/leadership/2010/speaker_zhao_xiao.asp.>.

Index

Abbreviation EMS stands for Executive Management Systems. Scriptural references using abbreviations KJV, NASB, NIV, and NLT refer to King James Version, New American Standard Bible, New International Version, and New Living Translation, respectively.

A

ABC's of brainstorming, 29

accountability. *See* personal accountability

achievement, overcoming obstacles, 40, 49–50, 56

active listening, 22–24

Akashi Kaikyo Bridge (Japan), 50

analytical thinking, 29

anxiety, x, 129–31

assumptions, 66–67, 68. *See also* values

autobiography, this book as, 155–56

awareness. *See* personal awareness

The Awesome Power of the Listening Ear (Drakeford), 22–23

B

Beaumont, George, 34

behaviors
defining culture, 68–73
linkage to values and leadership, 106–07, 155–56
values drive/create, 62–65

beliefs, defined, 67. *See also* values

benchmarks, life span/shared vision, 141–42

Bennis, Warren, 98

The Bible/Bible study, 130. *See also* Pathfinder verses; Scriptures

big picture/big-picture thinkers (generalists), 20, 25, 137–38

Brady, Chris, 82

brain function, right-/left-, 29

brainstorming, 29

brand identity/brand promise
action strategies, 15
creating EMS, 6–7
developing Mel Nelson as a, 8–11
importance of graphics in, 13–14

bridge-builder
skills and qualities, 39–40
vision of the future, 38–39
Winston Churchill as, 38

bridge/bridge-building. *See also* leadership; Mackinac Bridge; strategy; values; vision
achievement over obstacles, 49–50
as community unifier, ix–x
defined, 47
laws of physics and, 41–42
life span, 51–52
lifeline for communications, 48–49
as metaphor, vii, x–xi, 52–55
as model of business systems, 56
overcoming time and obstacles, 38–39, 46–48
role in life and business, 37–38
tragedy of failure, 45–46
as transition to the future, 95,

107, 109, 111–12, 120–21,
126, 128
bridges, structural components
cable anchorages, 53–55. *See
also* values
spans and road deck, 53–55.
See also strategy
suspension cables, 53–55. *See
also* leadership/leadership
skill
towers and footings, 53–55.
See also relationships
Bridges, William, 119
Brooklyn Bridge, 110–11
business model. *See also*
leadership; model/modeling;
relationships; strategy; values
about this book as, xiii
applying bridge metaphor,
53–55, 107, 126
creating a statement of
personal focus, 18–19
EMS as, 3–4, 14–15
using consultants, 42–44
*Business Model Innovation:
Proven Strategies That
Actually Work* (Butler, Butler
and Nelson), 90–93, 167
business strategy. *See also*
strategy
about using this book for, xiii
beginning the vision of EMS,
3–5
creating a brand identity, 8–
11
development of EMS role in,
5–7
EMS as facilitator of, 12–13
business systems, applying
bridge metaphor to, 56
Butler, Imelda, 89–92
Butler, John, 32, 89–93

C

cable anchorages. *See* values
The Centurion Principles
(O'Learey), 83
change leadership, process of,
118–21
children
coaching, 139–40
instilling discipline, 133–34
instilling values-driven
behavior, 62–65
living a shared vision with,
146–48
as mentors, 32
nurturing and guiding, 138
transition to adulthood, 139–
41, 144–45
Churchill, Winston, 38, 93, 128
coaching, 98–101, 103–07, 122,
139–40
Collier, Robert, 37
Collins, James C., 74
communication/communications
strategy
about fundamental skill of,
19–20
bridges as a lifeline, 48–49
creation of vision and focus,
18–19
listening ability/process, 22–
24
listening style, 24–26
questions and interactive
listening, 27–28
role of graphics in, 13–14
speaking/speaking ability, 21
writing and language skills,
21–22
confidence
coaching builds, 100–101
constructive criticism builds,
9
experience builds, 10–11
mentoring builds, 31–32
necessity for self-confidence,

assessing team skills, 100,
113–16
facilitating the process of,
29–31
strategic thinking and, 110
Inscape Publishing, 30
Institute of Electrical and
Electronic Engineers, 21
integrity
as basis of relationships, xiii
defined, 82–83
linkage of trust and honesty,
83–85
statement of core values, 74–
79
interactive listening. *See*
questions and interactive
listening
interpersonal relationships. *See*
relationships
"Is Your Business Model Right
for These Times?", 90–91

J

Johnson, Lyndon B., 23
justice, 76–78, 82

K

Kanter, Rosbeth Moss, 118
Kennedy, Robert, 118
The Key to Your Child's Heart
(Smalley), 131
A Kick in the Seat of the Pants
(von Oech), 30
Kotter, John P., 119–20
Kouzes, James M., 81
Kram, K. E., 33
Kublai Khan, xi

L

language skills. *See* writing and
language skills
*Launching a Leadership
Revolution: Mastering the Five
Levels of Influence* (Brady and

Woodward), 82–83
Lawrence, Paul R., 81
laws of physics, bridge-building
and, 41–42, 45–46
leadership. *See also*
bridges/bridge-building
applying bridge metaphor,
53–55, 95–97
as a bridge-builder tool, xiii,
39–42
developing confidence, 10–
11
emotional intelligence, 99–
100, 107
facilitation as fundamental
skill, 28–31, 34
failure, 94
leveraging diversity, 115–16
linkage to corporate ethics,
120–21
linkage to values and
behavior, 106–07, 155–56
listening is a, 22–27
Leadership Summit , Willow
Creek Association (2010), xiii
leadership development. *See also*
team engagement/team-
building
creating a personal vision,
103–05, 128
executive coaching and, 98–
99
for the "few" or the "many?",
97–98
identification of talent, 99–
100
linkage to values and
behavior, 106–07
private coaching, 100–101
3D Leadership Model, 88–89,
101–02
Levitlow, John J., 75
life coaching/life strategy, 104–
05
life model. *See also*
model/modeling; personal

14

responsibility, 76–78, 82, 88
Rockwell, Norman, 23
Romans 14:19 (NASB), 136
Rosenker, Mark, 45
Rosser, Manda H., 32–33

S

Schriever, Bernard A., 75
Schweitzer, Albert, 95
Scriptures (Biblical references).
See also God
    creating a Pathfinder list, 130
    Ecclesiastes 3:11 (NLT), 152
    Ecclesiastes 9:10a (NIV), 1
    Philippians 2:1-4 (NASB),
        137
    Philippians 4:8 (NASB), 137
    Proverbs 3:5-6 (NLT), 134
    Proverbs 22:6 (KJV), 64
    Proverbs 27:19 (NIT), 59
    Psalms 19:1 (NIV), 143
    Psalms 104:10 (NIV), 144
    Psalms 104:24 (NIV), 144
    Psalms 119:105 (NLT), 141–
        42
    Romans 14:19 (NASB), 136
    1 Thessalonians 5:11
        (NASB), 136
    1 Thessalonians 5:16-18
        (NASB), 137
*Secret Choices: Personal
    Decisions That Affect Your
    Marriage* (Wheat and Perkins),
    132–33
self-awareness. *See* 3D
    Leadership Model; personal
    awareness
self-doubt, 9
self-management. *See* 3D
    Leadership Model
self-pity, 129–31
self-respect, 76–78, 82
shared vision. *See also* personal
    reflections; vision

applying bridge metaphor,
    148–49
benchmarks, 141–42
business leadership/strategy,
    19, 116–18, 123–24
family legacy of, 149–52
husband-wife leadership,
    131–33
nurturing and guiding
    children, 133–34, 144–48
parental values, 63–65
Pathfinder scriptures for,
    136–38
reflections on living a life of,
    142–44, 152–53
statement of living a life of,
    135–36
Shelley, Kate, 48–49
simplicity, 17–19
situational awareness, 88
Smalley, Gary, 131
social awareness. *See* 3D
    Leadership Model
"social mirror", 8–9
speaking/speaking ability
    about the fundamental skill
        of, 21
    communications skills, 19–20
    keeping the words simple, 22
    strategic thinking and, 111–
        12
    use of mentors, 32
St. John, Matthew R., viii–xi
Steinman, David B., 40, 43, 109,
    110–11
"Stone Walls" (Croce), 5
strategic questions. *See* questions
    and interactive listening
strategic thinking/planning
    defined, 112
    EMS as facilitator of, 12–13
    importance of vision and
        focus, 18–19
    linkage to vision, 110–11
    test of verbalization, 111
strategy. *See also* bridges/bridge-

V

value proposition. *See* brand promise

values. *See also* bridges/bridge-building
  applying the bridge metaphor to, 53–55, 59–60, 78–79
  attributes of mentoring, 33
  defined, 65–67
  as a fundamental anchor, 60–61
  insights and reflections on, 61–65
  leadership responsibilities in, 69
  linkage to behaviors and leadership, 106–07
  linkage to faith and ethics, 156
  organizational/corporate culture, 67–69, 70–74
  role of discipline, 70

values statements/core values, 74–79

vision. *See also* bridges/bridge-building; goal-setting; personal reflections; shared vision
  applying bridge metaphor, 127–28
  beginning of EMS, 3–6
  as bridge to the future, 38–39
  creating a personal statement, 103–05
  escaping the rut of "success", 4–5
  execution strategy, 121–24
  focusing on a target market, 6–7
  linkage to strategic thinking, 110–12
  overcoming mediocrity, 3–4, 133
  overcoming time and obstacles, 46–48
  statement of core values, 74–79
  statement of personal focus, 18–19

von Oech, Roger, 30

W

Watson, Sara Ruth, 109

Westinghouse Electric Corporation, 21, 114, 166, 168

Wheat, Ed, 132

Willow Creek Association, xiii

wisdom and philosophy (Mel Nelson). *See also* personal reflections
  "experience is a better education than college...", 10
  "pay attention to your critics...", 9
  "take it or leave it" feedback, 9
  "there are 2 kinds of people...", 17
  understand the line between criticism and harassment, 9

Woodward, Orrin, 82

writing and language skills
  about the fundamentals of, 21–22
  keeping words simple, 22
  reflecting on one's own, 129
  use of mentors, 32

Z

Zenger, John H., 95

Melvin D. Nelson

As an author, speaker, business consultant and former senior energy and telecommunications executive, Melvin D. (Mel) Nelson brings thirty-five years of leadership experience to business owners and executives. He founded Executive Management Systems, Inc. in 2002 to share his expertise with business owners and executives: *Vision. Focus. Results.*

He was one of the executive team which created the Touchstone Energy® brand. Known internationally for his work in energy management, he was given the Nikola Tesla award by Westinghouse Electric Corporation for meritorious service to the electric power industry. As a registered professional engineer, he produced advertising, public relations programs and training videos which won prestigious national awards. He has led diverse groups of people in management and technical roles in operations, finance, marketing, and new business development.

Nelson, in his 40-plus-year business career, has always been a firm believer in the power of networking, and when he formed Executive Management Systems he made network development a priority. Today, Executive Management Systems is affiliated with nine international networks.

In 2007, he became affiliated with Odyssey Transformational Strategies, an international consulting network based in Dublin, Ireland. Nelson was at the table when the Top-Quartile Performance Institute (TQPI), also an international network of business consultants, was formed in April of 2011, with headquarters in Colorado Springs, Colorado. Nelson is one of five independent consultants tapped in 2010 to serve on the Odyssey Leadership Team, and he is also one of five consultants serving as thought-leaders guiding the development of the TQPI network.

Nelson is the author, along with John and Imelda Butler of Odyssey Transformational Strategies, of *Business Model Innovation: Proven Strategies That Actually Work*, published in 2010. His latest book – published in 2012 – is a more personal look at his "Building Bridges to the Future®" business model: *Building Bridges: Today's Decisions – Gateway to Your Future.*

Nelson has served on the board of governors of Trinity Western University, in Langley, British Columbia since 2004 and chairs the board development and governance committee.

Other Professional Experience

Nelson's proven corporate track record includes strategy development, marketing, corporate brand development, leading growth strategies, driving new business development, turning around an under-performing organization, and directing media and public relations during natural disasters and controversial events.

He served as the President and Chief Executive Officer at IdeaOne Telecommunications Group. Previously, he was with Minnkota Power Cooperative, Inc., as Vice President, Marketing & Public Relations. He produced numerous campaign materials including newsprint ads, videos, television commercials; and multi-state and national public relations programs. These were recognized with numerous national and international awards.

Mr. Nelson was one of twelve marketing executives elected nationally by energy suppliers to the Touchstone Energy Executive Council's Board of Directors. He led the strategic planning process for brand development that was adopted by Touchstone Energy. It formed the foundation for Touchstone's future success in becoming a national brand for the electric utility industry, encompassing over 600 energy suppliers.

Mr. Nelson managed an energy control center with professional staff including engineers, power system operators, engineering technicians and support staff. In this role, he directed power system operations for a regional power supplier serving 100,000 customers over a 35,000 square mile service area.

Working with associated energy suppliers, he directed the development of a world-renowned energy management program on a regional level. Mr. Nelson conducted global research, traveling to Switzerland, Belgium and Germany, studying various technologies. This innovative energy management program attracted global attention. Energy executives and senior engineers from Sweden, Germany, Switzerland, Japan, and Canada came to learn more about this leading-edge project. For his service to the electric power industry, Mr. Nelson was awarded the prestigious Westinghouse Nikola Tesla Award.

Mr. Nelson lives in North Dakota with his wife, a professional educator. They have three sons and one daughter, two daughters-in-law, one son-in-law, and six grandchildren. Maintaining an active lifestyle, Mr. Nelson frequently enjoys swimming and bicycling. He also enjoys hunting, fishing, backpacking, camping trips, and traveling with family and friends.